The

Winning Investor's
Guide to
Making Money
in Any Market

The
Winning Investor's
Guide to
Making Money
in Any Market

Andrew Horowitz, CFP

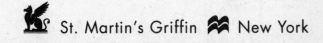 St. Martin's Griffin ≈ New York

www.stmartins.com

Text design by Meryl Sussman Levavi

Library of Congress Cataloging-in-Publication Data

Horowitz, Andrew.
   The winning investor's guide to making money in any market / Andrew
Horowitz.—1st ed.
        p. cm.
   Includes index.
   ISBN 978-0-312-55614-3
   1. Investments—Handbooks, manuals, etc.   2. Portfolio management—Handbooks,
manuals, etc.   3. Investment analysis—Handbooks, manuals, etc.   I. Title.
   HG4527.H668 2010
   332.6—dc22

                                                                        2010037790

First Edition: January 2011

10 9 8 7 6 5 4 3 2 1

Contents

Introduction

Unless you're independently wealthy and know your money will last for hundreds of years, you're like most of us: you're concerned about your financial security. You want to know how to invest your money so that you'll have enough money to retire comfortably, or send your kids to college, or leave a legacy, either to your family or the charities of your choice.

If you've gone online recently or to a bookstore or library, you know there are hundreds of books out there that go into extraordinary detail about different market sectors, investing strategies, and types of investments. There are books on technical analysis that are more than ten inches thick. There are also dozens of books on fundamental analysis. (If you're wondering what *that* is, I'll also explain what it is and how to do it—and I'll help you decide if it's the approach you want to take to manage your money.) In short, between all the financial newspapers, magazines, TV shows, and commentators, there's loads of information; trying to make sense of all of that information is like trying to take a sip of water out of an open fire hydrant.

Before you can begin to manage your money, however, you need to understand the basics. *The Winning Investor's Guide to Making Money in Any Market* isn't an exhaustive guide to everything you might ever want to know about investing; such a book would likely overwhelm you. Instead, this book provides the information you need to know—the quick and dirty tips—so you can get started investing your hard-earned money today and so you can make sure you have whatever you want or need for the rest of your life.

In the pages that follow I will give you the lowdown on some of the most important areas of investing. I will help you understand the tools and the lingo of investing so that you can get in the game. This book probably won't make you the next Warren Buffett. As you probably know, he's one of the most successful investors in history. What the book *will* do is give you a primer on the world of investing through my eyes. I've invested and managed other people's money (and my own)—successfully—for almost thirty years. I'm not an academic, and *The Winning Investor's Guide* isn't a textbook. I'm a Registered Investment Advisor (RIA) and a Certified Financial Planner (CFP)®, and I've helped thousands of individual clients (that is, people like you) and corporations define their investing strategies and grow their money so they can achieve their financial goals. I've been featured and quoted regularly on such media as CNBC, Bloomberg, CBS Market-Watch, Fox News, NPR, Reuters, the *New York Times*, the *Wall Street Journal*, *Barron's*, the *Financial Times*, the *Chicago Tribune*, and South Florida's *Sun-Sentinel*, to name just a few.

My colleagues and I at Horowitz & Company have seen some of the best of times in the world of investing, and we've seen some of the worst. More important, we eat our own cooking: we don't just offer advice on ways to invest successfully, we also follow it ourselves. I've written *The Winning Investor's Guide* to give you some quick and dirty tips about investing strategies that we have used successfully and to provide some insight into what makes a winning investor and how investing really works. Here I'll present the basic information and tools you need to make the smartest investing decisions. My advice is for anybody who wants to invest or is already investing—whether you're starting a 401(k) or you already have a 401(k); if you're just embarking on a career or you're about to retire; or if you are somewhere in between. Every once in a while, you may get a stock tip or some other investing advice, and if you want to know what to do with it, this book will help you decide.

What's in the Book?

Here's the game plan. First, I'll help you determine what kind of investor you want to be. In other words, how much time do you want to spend on investing, and how actively do you want to manage your investments? Then I'll go over the basics: the jargon and mumbo jumbo that you hear and read all the time, but may not completely understand. Next, armed with the basics, I'll help you overcome your fear of investing—or nervousness, or whatever emotions you may have. And we'll tackle that four-letter word that drives most investments, which, of course, is RISK. I'll also show you how to hedge your investments (like hedging your bets), an important strategy that can help you avoid massive losses no matter what you decide to invest in.

Next I'll describe some of the main economic indicators you should be watching in order to make reasonable decisions about what to invest in. I'll tell you what an indicator is, exactly which ones you should be watching, and where to find the info—quickly, since we're all about quick and dirty in this book—and how to use that information wisely.

I'll also share some game plans and strategies: how to invest when the market is trending down (I can hear you groaning, "Oh, no, will it ever come back?"); when the market is moving up (Dow 36,000, anyone?); and when the market is incredibly volatile. I'll clue you in on the top signals that will let you know the market is moving up—and the top signals the market is moving down. The book will help you to come up with ideas for what to invest in, and will explain how you can begin the investing process.

In the second half of *The Winning Investor's Guide*, I'll help you further investigate your initial investing ideas so you can identify which ones are the best. In doing so, I'll introduce the three main types of analysis investors use: quantitative analysis, fundamental analysis, and technical analysis. They're all valid but vastly different approaches to deciding what to invest in and how, so I'll first explain the differences among them and then demystify some of the terminology you may have heard. Then I'll explain how to put these different types of analysis all together.

In addition to covering what most people think of when they think of investing—stocks, bonds, and mutual funds—I'll also give you some quick and dirty tips on investing in less common, "alternative" investments: gold and other precious metals, food products and other commodities, foreign currencies, and real estate and REITs (real estate investment trusts). Finally, if you'd like more help than this book (or any other) can provide, I'll give some tips on how to choose a reputable and qualified financial advisor. And for a quick and dirty recall of the topics we've covered, there's a terrific glossary at the back of the book that can jog your memory about all the quick and dirty tips I'm offering.

Now let's get started!

PART I

Understanding the Basics

1

Getting Started

Step One: How Much Time and Energy Do You Want to Spend Managing Your Money?

The first thing you need to know about investing is that there are different ways to invest. When they hear the word *investing*, many people think of stocks only, not realizing that many other investment vehicles exist. I'll explain all of the basic options in chapter 2. Because there are so many options, the first decision you need to make is: how much time do you want to spend researching potential investments, choosing and deciding what to invest in, and managing your investments? Investing can be a full-time activity, or it can be something you do only part time. Only you can decide how many hours a day, a week, a month, or a year you will spend on your investments.

You may also decide to work with somebody else to come up with a game plan that meets your goals, and if that's the course you want to take, you can learn more about that in chapter 11, which will give you quick and dirty tips on choosing a reputable and qualified financial advisor. It's up to you to decide what kind of investor you are (or want to be), what exactly you want to do, and how much you want to be involved in managing and tracking your investments.

What Are Your Investment Goals?

Asking yourself why you want to invest may seem obvious, and if you're already clear on what your financial goals are in the short and long term, then feel free to skip this section. But if you haven't really thought about what you want to do with your money and when you will want to spend it, then you need to start thinking now. Time is critical when you're investing. If you need money tomorrow or within the next six months, you should probably be "investing" your money in cash, via a savings account, money market fund, certificate of deposit (CD), or short-term bond. On the other hand, if you're saving for retirement, then you have a much longer time frame—depending of course on how old you are and how close you are to retiring.

When you hear or use the word *invest*, don't confuse it with investing in company stocks only, which, as mentioned earlier, is what many people do. They think of investing only in terms of the stock market—that is, buying individual stocks, like Microsoft (MSFT), Pfizer (PFE), and so on. But investing encompasses so much more than just the stock market: you can invest in bonds, cash, mutual funds, ETFs (exchange-traded funds), and more—all of which I'll discuss in chapter 2.

We need to think of the word *investing* more along the lines of saving, preparing, and planning. In short, when you invest, you're simply putting money into something that you believe will pay off in the future. The first thing to determine—before you put any money anywhere—is how far into the future you're going to want to access that payoff, and what you're going to use it for.

Let's consider a few typical possibilities:

✦ Are you investing for your retirement?
  ◇ If so, when do you want to retire?
  ◇ How much money do you want to have (or do you think you'll need to have)?*
✦ Are you investing for your kids' college tuition? How far off is college? Are you the parent of a newborn, with seventeen years to accrue the money you'll need (though who knows what college will cost in seventeen years)? Or do you have thirteen-year-old triplets who want to go to Harvard, Yale, and Brown in five years?
✦ Are you investing so you can buy a house?
  ◇ If so, when do you want to buy? Again, your answer will affect whether your investments will be long-term (e.g., if you're twenty-one years old and want to buy a house by the time you're thirty) or short-term (e.g., if you want to buy a house within the next year).
  ◇ How much will you need for the down payment?

I realize these life goals require lots of self-knowledge and long-term planning—and you may have no idea yet what you want out of life, especially if you're relatively young. When the goals you're saving for, like buying a new house or retiring, are so far off, it can be hard to even think about investing, let alone actually do it.

---

*This is a tough question, even though there are myriad quick and dirty worksheets to help you calculate your retirement needs. If you're interested in mulling this problem further, take a look at *The Number: What Do You Need for the Rest of Your Life and What Will It Cost?* by Lee Eisenberg. Although this isn't a practical book (in that it doesn't tell you how to invest to attain that "number"), it is an intriguing book about one man's quest to figure out how much he and his family really need, and how much *you* might need as well, depending on what standard of living you're seeking in retirement.

One of my clients told me that when she was twenty-five, she didn't fully participate in her company's 401(k) plan because age sixty-five seemed like a lifetime away (and it was!). Plus she earned so little money that the thought of setting any of it aside was painful, and so she invested only the 2 percent of her salary that her company automatically set aside for her. After five years, her boss mentioned he had amassed $63,000 by investing the maximum allowable amount of 6 percent, with a matching contribution of another 6 percent from the company. During this time my client had accrued only $7,000. When she heard that her boss had accumulated enough for a healthy down payment on a house, she hightailed it down to Human Resources and increased the amount she invested. Fortunately, she was still young enough to save and invest wisely, and so twenty years later, she's very comfortable. That's an example of the power of the compound effect of interest—but you need to start young. Figuring out your goals is a good way to start.

Quick and Dirty Tip

Try to identify some financial goals, because *when* you want the money and *what* you want it for will direct how you invest. Write the goals down so you can refer to them later.

How to Figure Out Your Investing Goals

One of the most important goals you should have is to save enough to have the kind of retirement you want. Almost every investing Web site and periodical includes a tool or worksheet to help you calculate how much money you'll need to save. Most ask you a few questions to give you a ballpark estimate, such as:

✦ your age
✦ your annual salary
✦ how much you've saved for retirement in your 401(k), other savings, or both
✦ how much you save each month
✦ whether your investing style is aggressive, moderate, or conservative

Fidelity.com has a helpful interactive worksheet. You can get to it by clicking on "Guidance & Retirement," then on "Retirement," and then on "MyPlan Snapshot." Assuming you plan to retire at age sixty-five, the tool gives you two different amounts that it estimates you'll need for retirement:

✦ one amount based on the market performing poorly
✦ one amount based on the market performing on average

As mentioned, many other similar worksheets are available. A simple Google search for "retirement calculator" should help you find them.

Let's take a look at what a simple retirement calculator looks like.

Annual income required (today's dollars)	
Number of years until retirement	
Number of years required after retirement	
Annual inflation	
Annual yield on balance (percent) (fixed rate)	
Amount you'll need	

As you can see, the calculator asks you to input only a few variables:

✦ **Annual income required**: How much money do you think you'll need to live on each year, once you're retired?

✦ **Number of years until you retire**: This depends on your age. If you're thirty and plan to retire at sixty-five, then you have thirty-five years until retirement; if you're fifty-five and plan to work until you're at least seventy, then you have fifteen years; and so forth.

✦ **Number of years required after retirement**: This is, of course, a difficult question to answer because who knows? Give it your best conservative guess.

✦ **What you think the annual inflation rate will be**: This is another tricky number to estimate. In the 1970s, the inflation rate was above 7 percent, but during the first decade of the twenty-first century, it was below 3 percent. We can't know for certain what the rate will be, but for now let's use 4 percent.

✦ **Annual yield**: What interest rate do you expect (or hope) to receive on the money you've saved or invested?

Now, let's look at a popular retirement calculator from MSN Money at http://moneycentral.msn.com/retire/planner.aspx, where you can find and input your own variables.

It asks us a few more questions than the basics we just covered, such as how much money we have saved already, what our current salary is, and how much we are contributing to our retirement as a percentage of our salary. The MSN Money calculator assumes a 3 percent annual inflation rate, which is preset and you cannot change in the calculator.

Here's a sample calculator for Olivia, a single forty-five-year-old woman who already has $50,000 saved for retirement, plans to retire at age sixty-five, and guesses that she'll live until age eighty-five.

Age today	45
Age at retirement	65
My life expectancy	85
Annual income today	$60,000
Percentage saved for retirement each year	10 percent
Retirement savings today	$50,000
Average return on investments before retiring	7.0 percent
Anticipated return on investments after retiring	6.0 percent
How much I will need annually	$40,000
Other retirement income	$0
Include estimated social security benefit	yes
Annual withdrawal from savings:	$25,096
Savings at retirement	$295,000
Age when savings run out	79

After inputting the information, the calculator shows Olivia that after retiring, she'll be withdrawing over $25,000 each year from her savings and investments, which will be added to her other retirement benefits to receive $40,000 annually.

It also says that, assuming a 7.0 percent annual rate of return and that her 10 percent annual contributions continue, Olivia's retirement savings would grow to almost $295,000 when she turns sixty-five.

That number might initially sound great, but as you can see, the calculator also tells Olivia that her retirement savings would run out when she is seventy-nine years old—six years before she predicts she'll stop needing it. That tells her she'll need to adjust her savings or expected spending in retirement.

Let's say that she starts saving 15 percent of her income each year instead of the 10 percent that she does now. With that change, the calculator tells her that her retirement account is expected to grow to $386,000 when she retires at sixty-five. The calculator also now shows that she will run out of retirement savings at age eighty-five, which is what she input as her life expectancy. If she feels like she might live longer than that, she might try saving 16 percent or up to 20 percent of her annual salary.

Keep in mind that your salary will hopefully increase over the years. Though this sample calculator doesn't, some calculators allow you to input your expected percentage of salary increases each year, which may be 1 percent to 5 percent per year depending on your career.

Spend some time using different calculators and inputting different parameters. If you have a spouse, be sure to add his or her information into the calculations if you combine your retirement accounts. Some online calculators allow you to calculate individual information for your spouse as well.

This information can be very eye-opening, especially if you find out that you will not meet your retirement goals if you continue saving and investing as you do right now. Though learning this might be painful at first, it can help put you on the right path for a secure future.

Investing Helps You Achieve a Secure Future

Most of us want to have a secure future, and so we need to identify our goals now—particularly how much money we'll need for retirement—before we actually need that money and learn that we don't have enough. In addition to saving for retirement, you may have additional goals, such as saving to buy a house or paying for your child's education. It's not enough to simply wish for the best and hope that money will be there when you need it. Identifying your goals will enable you to put together the plan you need to reach them. And learning how to become a winning investor will help you achieve them.

Why Investing Today Is More Important Than Ever

The world has changed dramatically over the past few decades so that in terms of taking care of and planning for your own financial security, you really need to make your own way. Most companies used to provide retirement plans for their employees. Called *defined benefit plans*, they stated unequivocally (that's the *defined* part) what the company would pay you (that's the *benefit* part) when you retire. The plan would say something like "When you retire, you'll receive $2,000 a month from us for the rest of your life." (Of course, the final amount depended on annual salary and how many years the employee worked for the company.) Plus, there was Social Security income from Uncle Sam (more about that in a minute).

Around the mid-1980s, many companies changed their approach to employee retirement plans: they no longer offered the defined benefit plan. Instead, they started offering defined contribution plans, most often 401(k) plans—which required *you* to contribute to your own plan. In other words, you were now in charge of saving and investing for your own retirement, and the most your company would do was match a portion of your contributions.

All of a sudden, you're on your own: you are solely responsible for deciding how much of your paycheck you're going to save for retirement, and how you want to invest that money. So you'd better know what you're doing!

Even worse though, not only are you on your own, but in the wake of the financial meltdown of 2008, there aren't any guarantees that your employer will continue to make matching contributions; many companies have eliminated this benefit in order to save money. Now you're totally responsible for your future financial well-being.

In other words, over the last twenty years, retirement planning has changed completely. Whereas employees used to have a secure and planned retirement as part of an overall benefits package, now you can work for twenty or thirty years, getting your regular paycheck, but if you don't contribute financially to your retirement plan, you're not going to get anything on the way out.

In short, you need to figure out your financial future now, because more than ever before *you* are responsible for your own personal finances, your own personal stability, and your future. You need to plan as if nobody is going to be there to support you.

To add more salt to your financial wounds, we can't even say whether Social Security will be available when we retire. If you're a young person—or even if you're in your forties or fifties—you can't count on receiving it. For most of us (unless you're close to age sixty-five), Social Security is just a vanishing mirage. Of course, we continue to receive annual updates from Uncle Sam, indicating how much we should receive when we retire, but we certainly can't depend on that money, because it is possible that the system will eventually be bankrupt.

Here it is, in a nutshell: you have to be that much smarter about how you're investing because you're bearing all the risk and responsibility for your investments. Thus it is very important to know what you're doing. You can no longer just make assumptions and believe that the future is going to be a certain way. The world has changed too much. That doesn't necessarily mean that it's worse, but it has changed, and so you need to be more adept in understanding investments and how they work.

How Much Time Do You Want to Spend on Your Investments?

Essentially, there are two types of investors: passive and active. However, there are degrees of each, and I tend to think of them on a continuum, as shown in the accompanying diagram. Let's look at each investor type in terms of how much time and energy each is putting into investing.

What Type of Investor Are You?

Superpassive   Passive   Fairly Active   Active   Superactive

Superpassive Investors

If you plan to check on your investments and to consider changing your portfolio, or collection of investments, once or twice a year, then you're a *superpassive investor*. There are tens of millions of people just like you. Superpassive investors are often people who invest for the long term primarily through their 401(k), 403(b), IRA, or other retirement account; in other words, they don't have any other type of investment, such as an individual brokerage account. This group really doesn't want to research specific stocks, bonds, or alternative investment opportunities, so they simply invest in mutual funds or exchange traded funds (which I'll talk more about in chapter 2).

Here's an example of a superpassive investor: Cami is forty-five years old, and she has a good job, where she works a regular eight-hour day. She has a decent 401(k) plan that she's been contributing to since she graduated from college and got her first job. She's also married, with four children. She and her husband Fred have decided they don't want to spend a lot of time reading financial newspapers and magazines or watching financial news commentators on TV who are espousing their view of the markets. But Cami and Fred do want to invest for their kids' college educations and for their eventual retirement.

Therefore Cami and Fred have decided to invest in mutual funds and ETFs (we'll discuss these in chapter 2, or you can turn to the glossary for quick and dirty definitions). Cami and Fred are traditional "buy-and-hold" investors; in other words, they plan to hold on to whatever they buy for a long time. They're not going to track the price of what they've bought today so that they can sell at a profit tomorrow, or next month, or even next year. They're trusting that they'll earn money over the long haul.

The Buy-and-Hold Investing Strategy

Buy-and-hold is a popular strategy for many investors, including the famed Warren Buffett. Buffett, whose approximate net worth is $47 billion, made his money solely by investing. Although he's hardly a passive investor, his long-term investing strategy fits that of a passive investor. There have been dozens of books written about him and his investing strategy, based on his preferred investing time frame, which he says is "forever." His attitude is, "I've invested in a quality company, so why should I get rid of that investment?"

Buffett's strategy can certainly work if you have a long enough time frame. All things considered, a broad-based and well-researched diversified investment portfolio can do well over many years, so you don't have to watch over your investments every minute. In fact, the buy-and-hold strategy has also been called the "Sleeping Beauty" portfolio, because you essentially go to sleep for many years, hoping that you've chosen your investments wisely, and then you wake up and see if your investments have paid off as you planned and hoped.

Keep in mind that Buffett is really in a class by himself as an investor, because he doesn't simply invest in companies the way the average investor does. Instead, he frequently buys entire companies so that he has direct control over how they are run, so in those companies, he is more of an owner-investor.

The problem with the Sleeping Beauty strategy is it doesn't work if you don't have a long enough time frame. Suppose Cami, our superpassive investor, followed her buy-and-hold approach. She was forty-five when she started and is sixty-six today, retired, and drawing income from her hard-earned retirement money. Let's say she retired in early 2010. In that case, Cami, as Sleeping Beauty, would have awakened in 2010 ready to use her investment money for retirement . . . but, unfortunately, she lost out because she happened to be born on the wrong date. In other words, because Cami retired at a time when the market wasn't doing so well, her investments—when she needed to start using them—were worth much less than she thought they would be. It wasn't her fault, of course, because she did all the things she was told to do.

Now how do you get around that? That's the $64 billion question: what can Cami do *now*? There are many people just like our fictional Cami who are facing this very same concern.

In the aftermath of the stock-market meltdown of 2008 and others throughout the last century, it's my opinion that the buy-and-hold strategy needs to be requestioned. I firmly believe it's no longer a good idea to simply put your money into some investment, let it sit there for decades, and accept that whatever happens, happens. That's a lazy portfolio, if you will—and it can have a very detrimental effect on your financial security and well-being. If you choose to be a superpassive investor, just be aware of the risks involved.

Passive Investors

If you're spending, or planning to spend, about five hours a month on investing, you're still a *passive investor*. Five hours a month isn't enough time to keep on top of everything you need to be researching, watching, thinking about, and deciding on. It's not enough time for you to be considered an active investor. Again though, there are millions of people like you, and you just need to know how to make the best use of the time you *do* spend on investing.

Here's another example: Adam, who is fifty-two years old, runs his own business, which means he has a demanding workload consuming long hours. He's also married to Judy and has a couple of kids, and he wants to spend most of his spare time with his family. He's willing to spend an hour or so every weekend keeping up on what he needs to know to ensure his family's financial security.

That "hour or so" once a week, however, adds up to only about five hours a month, which isn't enough time for Adam to actively manage his investments—or for you to manage yours. Although Adam wants to have a cursory understanding of the financial markets, his investments, and the risks he's taking, he also decides to hire a professional financial manager or advisor (which I'll discuss in chapter 11). Because working with a financial advisor means Adam will be checking in with and meeting with this advisor—which of course takes time—Adam isn't a superpassive investor like Cami; he's a passive investor.

To sum up, passive investors may spend about five hours a month on their investments by handing them off to somebody else or by having a fairly lazy portfolio. Then they can focus on their main business or job, where they'll make most of their money. If you're a passive investor, then you probably have something to do in life that you consider more important than actively managing your investments. All you really want to do is check your statements every so often, read the financial news on a daily basis, listen to an occasional financial news program on radio, TV, or a podcast, and talk to your advisor perhaps a few times a quarter. It will be your advisor who will be doing the heavy lifting of researching possible investments for you and monitoring your existing investments to make sure they help you reach your financial goals.

Fairly Active Investors

Unlike passive investors, *fairly active investors* really want to get involved in investing. They are willing to spend a half hour or so a day to monitor their investments, looking at ideas for new investments they might want to research, and checking up on how their current investments are doing.

For this example, Danielle, in her thirties (although age is not a determining factor), simply has more energy and time than our earlier investors, Cami and Adam. She's single, with no children, and although she works long hours at a demanding job, she still has time to research and monitor her investments. Danielle either devotes 30 minutes a day, 7 days a week, to this or else spends 3½ hours doing so on the weekend.

Either way, that's certainly enough time for her to scan *Barron's* or look at the recommendations of *Investor's Business Daily*, which has a great list of highly rated stocks and mutual funds that she might want to research further. She might also read other financial newspapers and magazines to get ideas for possible investments, review her portfolio, and sketch out an idea a week for an investment she wants to review further. (We'll cover analysis and research in Part II.) Unlike Adam, Danielle doesn't want to leave the decision of what investments are in her portfolio to her money manager, and unlike Cami, she doesn't want to just hope her investment choices do well in the long run. She therefore sets aside at least 3½ hours a week to discover new investing opportunities that she believes may help to increase the value of her portfolio.

Active Investors

If 3½ hours a week isn't enough time for you to monitor and manage your investments, then you might want to be an *active investor*: someone who spends about three hours a day reading, researching, and investing.

For example, Karen, who is forty years old and works an eight-hour day, has free time in the morning before work and in the evening, which she chooses to *not* spend watching TV, socializing, or indulging in any other leisure activities. Instead, Karen is willing to devote 3 to 4 hours a day on her investments. She probably spends 1½ hours in the morning looking at what her investments are doing, monitoring the markets, and reading the financial news. She looks to see if there's anything she might want to buy or sell. Then at the end of the day, she'll review what happened, where the markets closed, and what additional news came out. She can then follow up on daily trends.

Karen reads several investment newspapers and magazines, watches financial news shows, and listens to investment podcasts, just to get ideas for what to research further and consider investing in. She also spends time analyzing those potential investments by doing either fundamental or technical analysis (which we'll cover in Part II) to determine whether the preliminary investing ideas she's gotten from her research are really worth sinking her hard-earned money into. Of course, she needs to monitor the investments she decides to make, which may lead her to buying and selling more often. That is why she's an *active* investor. Karen wants to make sure she's not missing out on any great investment opportunities or holding on to something, like a falling stock, when she should be getting rid of it.

Active investors are people who want to be involved, have more of an interest in money management, and maybe even want to supplement their incomes with trading or investing. These people have a much greater intellectual commitment to investing, and generally they are willing to devote a great amount of time to it. That may be the amount of time *you* want to devote to your investments too.

Superactive Investor

If you think three hours a day still isn't enough time for you to read, watch, research, and monitor, you may want to be a *superactive investor*. One such investor—I'll call him Mike—is likely *not* working at another job, at least not full-time, but he is willing to devote himself full-time to his investments, spending about eight hours a day, five days a week. In other words, the superactive investor is going to be thinking about his investments all day. Mike might be a professional money manager like me, who's managing money not only for himself but also for other people, his clients.

However, Mike is not a day trader. There is a difference between superactive investing and day trading. Investing is the art of buying stock, bonds, real estate, or any other type of investment because you believe it's going to do well over time, even though there may be hiccups here and there. Over time, you believe that a stock, for example, is going to do well, and so you want to be invested in that, you want to hold on to it. I don't call this buy-and-hold necessarily; instead, what you're doing when you're investing is taking a position that you're willing to hold on to over time because your research shows that this will be a good longer-term opportunity for yourself.

How Active Do You Want to Be?

Now that you know the amount of time involved in each approach to investing, take a look at the spectrum again, and decide where you want to be.

What Type of Investor Are You?	How Much Time Do You Spend on Investing?
1. Superpassive	You review investments once or twice a year.
2. Passive	You review investments about five hours per month, but you also work with a financial advisor.
3. Fairly active	You read, review, and research thirty minutes a day or three-and-a-half hours a week.
4. Active	You read, review, and research three hours a day.
5. Superactive	You read, review, and research eight hours a day, five days a week, focusing on medium- to long-term investments.

Do you want to buy and hold for the long, long term? Or do you want to be in and out of the market, attempting to time it so that you're buying and selling and trying to make money all the time? Some people want to invest because they believe it's easy—they think, "Look, the market goes up and down; I can make money and it's a quick buck." Their attitude often changes very quickly though when they have to put their own money on the line and decide, "Do I stay in? Is the market going down more? Should I put more money into this investment? Is the market going up? Do I want to change something?"

That's why the first big questions you need to answer are: Do you want to manage your own money? How much involvement do you want to have? Do you want somebody else to manage your money? Do you want to be checking on your positions on a daily basis? Do you want your portfolio to include individual stocks, mutual funds, or ETFS? How much money do you want to risk? How much money and time do you want to spend on research?

Answering these questions will lead you to conclude how you're going to handle investing. Let's say that you want to be involved, at least involved enough to be knowledgeable about your investments and to understand what's going on. Maybe you don't want to know the finer details, but you do want to understand things like "Why am I invested in this market sector (such as technology or health care or manufacturing)? Why is this happening to my investments? What should I be doing?" There are newsletters that you can subscribe to, which provide good tips and give you good research and rankings on investments. There are hedge funds. There are investment advisors. There are mutual funds. (I'll explain these terms in the next chapter.) There's a whole host of investing choices you can make.

Basically, I believe your decision depends on this: what is the most important thing in your life? Is it important to be with your family? to do well in your job? Is it important to be involved in your community? With your answers in mind, you can decide whether you have time to devote to your investments. Again, it boils down to how much time you want to spend and what you find fun in life.

I do think it's important, no matter what your circumstances, that you spend at least some time, have at least some information, and have at least some relationship with your investments. It's not a good idea to just ignore them.

If, after reading this chapter, you've decided you just want to check in once a quarter, once every six months, or once a year, I recommend you proceed with caution. Many people believe the markets, over time, will be higher, but you're taking on a great deal of risk by checking your investments infrequently.

If you want to spend less than five hours a month on investing and if you simply want to understand the basics of investing, then you're a passive investor. I believe you should consider hiring a professional money manager or financial advisor whom you can rely on and trust. I also strongly believe that your money means more to *you* than to anybody else in the world, so you need to take some responsibility for it, even with a money manager. I'll talk more about money managers in chapter 11.

On the other hand, if you're the type of person who likes to get into detail and reading/researching/monitoring is something you want to do, I think you should choose to be a fairly active investor. Read as much as you can and understand that some "information" is just PR and thus not objective. It's a good idea to keep your finger on the pulse of blogs, podcasts, radio, TV, newspapers, and so on. If you want to be an active or superactive investor and do a lot of analysis, you should consider investing in individual stocks (described in more detail in chapter 2). Keep in mind that you don't want to bite off more than you can chew, because we're talking about real money; investing is not a game that uses Monopoly money. Also, you don't want to set yourself up for failure. Don't start investing and then ignore your investments, and don't hand off your money to someone else and not pay attention to how that person is investing it. Again, it's your money, and you don't want to lose it.

2

The Basic Investing Vehicles

Stocks, Bonds, Mutual Funds, Exchange-traded Funds,

Foreign Investments, and Currency Transactions

As mentioned in chapter 1, when people hear the word *investing*, many of them think only of the stock market. Though stocks are one way to invest your money, there are many other investing vehicles you can choose from to meet your financial goals. In this chapter I will present the information you need to know about the four basic investing vehicles: stocks, bonds, mutual funds, and ETFs, and I will go over some jargon you hear all the time but may not completely understand. Let's start off by tackling a common investing term you've probably heard many times: *diversification*.

What Is Diversification?

One reason it's important to know about all the available investment options is for diversification. Simply put, *diversification* is a way to manage risk (which I'll get to in chapter 3) by spreading it out among multiple investments in your portfolio. It could mean holding different kinds of stocks instead of just one—for instance, a bunch of retail stocks (Target [TGT], Tiffany's [TIF]) in addition to technology stocks (Apple [AAPL], Microsoft [MSFT]). Diversification could also mean investing in bonds or mutual funds in addition to stocks. That way, if one type of investment loses money, you have other types of investments that are hopefully making money and balancing out the loss. Think of your investment portfolio as a garden. If you grow only impatiens, your garden will be beautiful for three months of the year. Unfortunately, impatiens die off, leaving you with a mulch pile for the rest of the year. In order to have a beautiful garden year-round, you want to grow not just impatiens, but also roses, heliconia, evergreens, and so forth. In other words, you want to have something blossoming all the time. The same is true of your portfolio. If certain investments aren't doing well, you want to make sure that other investments you hold are.

Okay, now you understand why it's important to know about more than just stocks. Let's get on with our discussion of the different investing vehicles. We'll start by describing the quick-and-dirty of what you need to know about each vehicle.

The Four Main Investment Vehicles

As mentioned, the most common investing vehicles are stocks, bonds, mutual funds, and ETFs.

+ **Stocks:** A stock is an ownership interest in a company. For example, if I have a lemonade stand and I realize I need more money to run it, I can sell "shares"—that is, stock—in my lemonade stand. Each share is a piece of the business that every shareholder (or stockholder) owns. So when you buy stock in a company, you have part ownership of that company.

✦ **Bonds:** A bond is an IOU. Let's use the same lemonade stand example. As the owner, I obviously need to buy lemons, and I need to advertise, both of which require money. If I don't want to sell shares, or stock, in my lemonade stand, I can either go to a bank and borrow that money, or I can approach the public and ask them to lend me the money. Approaching the public for a loan is essentially what a bond sale is. When you as an investor buy a bond, you're actually lending your money to a company or to a government (we'll cover types of bonds later in this chapter). You make this loan in return for a promise from the company (in this case, Lemonade Stand, Inc.) to pay back the loan at some date in the future, together with the interest on that loan. The interest is how you, the investor, make money on the deal.

✦ **Mutual funds:** A mutual fund is an investment in which shareholders pool their money with the intent of investing in a diversified portfolio of securities (that is, stocks, bonds, or almost anything that represents financial value). Instead of having to research and choose specific stocks, bonds, or other investing vehicle, you pool your money along with others into a conglomeration of investments that are chosen and managed by a professional mutual fund manager.

✦ **Exchange-traded Funds (ETFs):** One of the four main investing vehicles. It is similar to a mutual fund in that it's made up of different securities, but it is also different because it trades like a stock on an exchange. ETFs are more flexible than mutual funds because you can buy and sell shares of ETFs throughout the day, taking advantage of inter-day changes in the market. ETF fees are often lower than mutual fund fees because most ETFs don't need to be actively managed.

Let's take a closer look at how to invest in each type of investing vehicle, beginning with stocks and the stock markets.

Stocks

Stocks are bought and sold, or traded, on a stock market. The term *stock market* is actually a misnomer because there are several different markets, all of which I'll describe in this chapter. For a quick and dirty overview though, you should know that in the United States stocks are usually bought and sold either on the New York Stock Exchange (NYSE), on the NASDAQ, or via ECNs (electronic communications networks, where individual investors can trade directly with a major brokerage house without working through a middleman). Every available stock is bought or sold through different markets. Some stocks are available through more than one market, whereas others can only be bought through one.

Trading on the stock market means that you're buying a number of shares in a company that you think will eventually be worth more money. For example, if you like Starbucks (SBUX) coffee and you think the company makes a good product that will continue to sell well and realize a profit, then you may want to buy stock in Starbucks. Of course, investing in stocks can be a lot more complicated than that, but that's the basics of the transaction. You buy shares in a company today that you believe will be worth more in the future when you sell your shares.

New York Stock Exchange and the NASDAQ

As I mentioned, two of the biggest markets in the United States are the New York Stock Exchange and the NASDAQ. The New York Stock Exchange (NYSE) is an actual place; it's in Lower Manhattan. It's an auction-based exchange, where specialists in specific stocks take orders for buying and selling shares.

NASDAQ (pronounced *naz-dack*) stands for the National Association of Securities Dealers Automated Quotations, although you'll never hear it referred to by its full name. The NASDAQ, which was created in 1971, differs from the New York Stock Exchange in that it's an electronically traded market and not a physical location. In other words, there are no people standing at a NASDAQ place waving their hands, buying and selling like they do on the floor of the New York Stock Exchange. Instead, the NASDAQ is a network of computers that are connected through servers, which allow the matching of orders. One person buys; another sells. All you need is a computer, and you can electronically buy and sell shares in stocks yourself.

The NYSE currently comprises about 2,800 stocks, and the NASDAQ comprises about 3,800 stocks. Traditionally, a stock that's traded on the NYSE is abbreviated with one to three letters—for example, IBM. Companies listed on the NASDAQ are abbreviated with at least four letters, such as AAPL for Apple.

Just as the United States has its stock markets, other countries around the world have their own markets too. There are stock exchanges in Hong Kong, London, Frankfurt, Istanbul, Shanghai, Singapore, Tel Aviv, Tokyo, and many others places.* They aren't traded as actively by most U.S. investors, though I'll tell you a little about them anyway later on. In addition, you should know that when most people talk about "the market," they probably are referring to the Dow Jones Industrial Average (DJIA) or the S&P 500, both of which are known as indexes.

---

*For a complete list of the 52 regulated international stock exchanges, see the World Federation of Exchanges at www.world-exchanges.org or Stock Exchanges Worldwide Links at www.tdd.lt/slnews/Stock_Exchanges/Stock.Exchanges.htm.

Stock Indexes

An *index* is a grouping of stocks that have certain similar character-istics and can be tracked as one unit. An index can be made up of companies from a specific sector (health care, real estate, etc.), or a specific market size (generally referred to as market capitalization), or a certain geographic area, or type of investment (an index of value stocks, an index of growth stocks). Two of the main U.S. stock indexes are the Dow Jones Industrial Average and the S&P 500. Though you can't actually purchase an index, you can invest in funds, such as ETFs, that mirror the performance of certain indexes.

Stock indexes have another benefit, too. Tracking them is a way to evaluate how your investments are doing. If your invest-ments consistently lag behind certain key indexes, then it might be time to make some changes.

Dow Jones Industrial Average (DJIA)

When you hear newscasters talk about how the Dow is doing, they are referring to the Dow Jones Industrial Average, or DJIA. The Dow, which comprises thirty stocks, is one of the most widely fol-lowed stock indexes in the world. The Dow is named after Charles Dow, who was a cofounder of Dow Jones & Company, a publish-ing and financial information firm started in 1882. Though the word *Industrial* is in its name, today the DJIA includes companies from many sectors of the economy; financial services such as Amer-ican Express (AXP), restaurants such as McDonald's (MCD), technology such as Microsoft (MSFT), pharmaceuticals like Pfizer (PFE), and retail like Walmart (WMT).

The Dow is important for two reasons. First, despite consist-ing of only thirty companies' stocks, the Dow tracks how the stock market overall is doing. It's a benchmark. If you watch the news, you've probably heard commentators say things like "The Dow just passed 10,000." That "10,000" is a dollar amount, and it's simply the sum of the current stock price of the thirty companies comprising the DJIA, divided by what's called the Dow divisor. (The divisor is too complicated to explain here, and fortunately not necessary for you to know in order to invest well!) The higher the stock prices of the thirty companies are, the higher the Dow and the stronger the stock market is. But don't look at the Dow as representative of the performance of the stock market as a whole, because it includes only a handful of stocks. In other words, the Dow is a good thing to look at but not to live by.

The second reason the Dow is important is that you can invest in it. One way to do that is with ETFs, and I'll discuss that later in this chapter.

The S&P 500

The S&P 500 is another closely watched stock index. S&P stands for Standard & Poor's. In the 1920s, the Standard Statistics Company developed its first stock-market indicator, and in 1941, Standard Statistics merged with Poor's Publishing—hence the name Standard & Poor's. The S&P 500 index itself was created in 1957, years after the two companies merged.

Like the Dow, the S&P 500 is an index or, essentially, a group of stocks. Because the S&P 500 index is made up of stocks from 500 companies, it's much more representative of the stock market as a whole than the Dow is. The S&P 500 traditionally consists of large, well established companies, and it includes many of the popular and well-known stocks that are generally traded, such as Aetna Insurance (AET), DuPont Chemicals (DD), Hasbro toys (HAS), Macy's Department Stores (M), PepsiCo (PEP), Sherwin-Williams (SHW), and Yahoo! (YHOO). Many portfolio managers, investment advisors, and mutual fund managers use the S&P 500 as a benchmark to compare how their specific investments are doing. For example, if the S&P 500 index is up 5 percent, and your investment in Coca-Cola (KO) is up 10 percent, then you're doing better than the S&P 500 index (assuming that Coca-Cola is your only investment).

Aside from being an excellent broad-based U.S. index to watch, there are also mutual funds and ETFs that replicate the S&P 500 list. I'll talk more about them a little later.

How Else Are Stocks Categorized?

In addition to being grouped into different indexes, stocks can also be categorized in various other ways. For example, some stocks are categorized by their company's market capitalization, which is one way to measure the value of a company.

Large-, Mid-, Small-, and Micro-Cap Companies

Market capitalization is the value of the number of outstanding shares of a company's stock—that is, the total number of shares that have been issued and are owned by the public, multiplied by the company's current stock price. For example, if a company has one million outstanding shares trading at $1 per share, then the company is market capitalized at $1 million. That market capitalization will change, of course, if the number of outstanding shares changes (for example, if the company releases more shares) and as the stock price changes. Companies are often divided into different groups based on their market capitalization, as follows.

+ **Large-cap companies** are usually valued at more than $5 billion. These are often older, more stable companies such as McDonald's (MCD), IBM (IBM), Microsoft (MSFT), 3M (MMM), and Procter & Gamble (PG)—in other words, all the megacompanies.
+ **Mid-cap companies** are valued at about $1 billion to

$5 billion, which obviously is still fairly huge, so "mid-cap" is somewhat of a misnomer. Mid-cap companies include Panera Bread (PNRA); Smithfield Foods (SFD), which makes pork products; Wendy's fast-food restaurants (WEN); Timberland (TBL); Plantronics (PLT), which makes headsets for phones; and Netflix (NFLX).

+ **Small-cap companies** are usually valued between $500,000 and $1 billion. The Kirby Company (KEX), which makes vacuum cleaners; Carter's (CRI), which makes children's clothes; Jack in the Box (JACK); and Ruby Tuesday's (RT) are examples of small-cap companies.

+ **Micro-cap companies** are the smallest, typically under $250 million, in market capitalization. As a result, some investors don't even look at these companies; they're so small that most people have never even heard of them.

We often find that the best stocks to invest in are mid-cap stocks. Mid-cap companies are just breaking out of the small-cap classification and potentially have great futures. Why? Because they're not fully mature yet, meaning they still have an opportunity to grow. More investors are starting to notice mid-cap companies, and as more investors buy, the price of mid-cap stocks goes up. That said, you often get the greatest bang for the buck by investing in micro- or small-cap companies that have a product or service that breaks out and does extraordinarily well. For instance, Microsoft (MSFT) started as a small-cap company; then it "grew up," because, over time, more shares were issued, there were stock splits*, and its price went up. But investing in micro-cap or small-cap companies

*The stock price got so high that the company cut the price in half, making each share worth 2 shares. For example, if you held 50 shares of a stock priced at $100, and the stock split, you would then own 100 shares of the stock, now priced at $50 per share.

carries the most risk. For every Microsoft or Apple success story, there are hundreds of not-so-successful companies whose share-price value declined or was even delisted when the company declared bankruptcy. Knowing where your stock fits in the market-cap universe is important for diversification. You don't want your whole portfolio to be in any one group, or you won't be properly diversified.

Quick and Dirty Tip

You have the potential to make the most money over time with successful small- and mid-cap companies, but they are much more risky than large-cap competitors. The share prices of most large-cap companies are more stable over time so they carry less risk, but investors often trade off profit potential for safety.

Growth Stocks Versus Value Stocks

In addition to being grouped according to index and market capitalization, stocks can also be grouped as *growth stocks* and *value stocks*. Growth stocks are typically more earnings-based, which means that when investors look at them, they look to the ongoing growth of earnings rather than the overall stability of the company. Growth stocks will continue to have very strong growth in revenues and in earnings, or profits. Typically, you find earnings-based stocks in companies in the technology and health-care industries.

In contrast, value stocks are generally companies in the financial industry and in utilities. Value stocks are from companies with a high book value, which is simply the company's assets minus its liabilities (discussed in chapter 8). Their earnings might not be steadily growing, but quality companies should be profitable.

Value stocks tend to pay dividends, which are payments generally given quarterly to shareholders as a way for companies to "share" their profits.

There are growth and value companies in each of the sizes of market capitalization. For example, there are large-cap value stocks and there can be small-cap growth stocks.

It's often beneficial to diversify your portfolio between growth and value investments because they don't always have the same returns during the same period. In other words, they cycle. There can be a time when growth stocks are in favor (for example, during a big boom market), and if you've invested in them, you will often do very well and make money. Conversely, there can be a time when value stocks are in favor (for example, during a flat market), and if you've invested in these stocks, then you should do very well and make money, due to dividends and price stability. Therefore you should diversify by investing in both growth and value stocks so that you're not dependent on the success of only one type.

Bonds

As mentioned earlier, bonds are like IOUs. When you buy a bond, you're lending your money to a company or government in exchange for its promise to pay you back at some future date, together with the interest on that loan. You make money by earning the interest. A bond matures, or comes due, a certain amount of time after it's issued; that time period is set by the issuer. A bond's maturity can vary from as little as six months (that is, you buy it on January 1 and it reaches full value on July 1) to thirty years (for example, your grandparents gave you a bond when you were born, and on your thirtieth birthday, that bond matures). Usually, the longer the term, or time period, the more interest you'll earn.

There are many different types of bonds. These include U.S. Treasury bonds, municipal bonds, corporate bonds, and junk bonds.

U.S. Treasury Bonds

U.S. Treasury bonds are sold by the federal government. Some Treasury bonds have minimum investment requirements—for example, $1,000, $2,000, $10,000. You can buy these directly from Treasury Direct at www.treasurydirect.gov. Long-term Treasury bonds are considered the safest in the world—or at least they were until the global meltdown of 2008.

Municipal Bonds

In addition to U.S. Treasury bonds, other government bonds are issued, or sold, by state municipalities. These are municipal bonds, which investment professionals often call "munis." *Municipal bonds* are usually tax-free on the federal level, which means you don't have to pay federal taxes on the income you earn from them.

There are two different kinds of municipal bonds: *general obligation* and *revenue*. General obligation bonds are secured by a local government's guarantee to use legally available resources, such as taxes, to repay bondholders. These bonds are backed by the full taxing authority of the state or the municipality issuing them, so if the government doesn't have enough money to pay back the bond, the state or municipality can raise the taxes paid by its taxpayers. As simple as that sounds, it's not easily done, because raising taxes is unpopular, and politicians don't want to be voted out of office at the next election.

Revenue bonds, on the other hand, repay bondholders based on the income generated from things like tolls on bridges, tunnels, highways, or other projects. If that bridge or tunnel isn't making enough to pay the interest on the bond, then the toll prices need to be increased. But what if people won't pay the higher prices? That's a problem. Traditionally, general obligation bonds have been considered safer because they are supported by the full taxing power of a municipality. However, that's not always true. Revenue bonds are much more flexible than they used to be, because municipalities can adjust their rates much more readily than local governments can adjust their overall tax rate. Still, one type is not really "safer" than the other right now, and so you'll have to evaluate each bond on an individual basis. Keep in mind that both carry a risk of default.

Though muni bonds carry a risk of default, you can protect yourself with a kind of insurance unique to municipal bonds: it guarantees that your principal and all associated interest will be repaid in the event of default. Bond issuers buy such insurance to enhance their credit rating by reducing the amount of interest they need to pay and to make the bonds more attractive to investors. With this type of insurance, you can take comfort in the fact that you bought an insured bond and that it's rated higher because the insurance company has (supposedly) investigated it thoroughly. The insurance company doesn't want to lose its money either. Timely payment of interest and principal is guaranteed by the municipality and the insurance company, so if the municipality goes under, you have some protection if you own an insured bond.

One last note about muni bonds: if you're considering buying state bonds, remember that different states make their money in different ways. For example, Florida has no income tax, so it's earning money from real estate, travel, tourism, and so on. However, if the country is in a recession, it's likely that these industries aren't doing so well, and so the state's budget may have problems. That means it might not be the smartest idea for you to buy muni bonds from Florida, because in a very extreme instance the situation could get so bad that the state might not be able to pay back its bonds. In contrast, New York has a very high income tax, and because the state can levy a tax on its residents, its bonds might be a safer bet. Understand too that a municipality can go bankrupt. Although it is rare, it can happen: New York City nearly went bankrupt during the 1970s. The bottom line here is before you consider muni bonds, think long and hard about which states you are considering. And consider diversifying your municipal bond portfolio so that you don't only hold bonds from a single state.

Corporate Bonds and Junk Bonds

In addition to U.S. government bonds and municipal bonds, you can also invest in *corporate bonds*. These bonds are offered by corporations, and they come in different qualities, if you will, depending on the financial strength of the company itself. In other words, there are high-quality corporate bonds and lower-quality corporate bonds, all the way down to what are known as junk bonds.

Junk bonds, which are below investment grade, often provide a higher interest rate than you would get on higher-quality bonds. An "investment grade" bond is one that has been rated highly by bond ratings organizations, so it has a relatively low risk of default. In contrast, a bond that is below investment grade has a higher risk of default—hence the name "junk bonds." Although junk bonds may return higher interest rates, junk bonds are riskier; you could lose your money if the issuing company defaults. As is often the case with most investments, the higher the possible return on your investment, the higher the risk you'll have to bear. This is a theme you'll wrestle with throughout your investing life: you have to achieve a reasonable balance between risk and reward. Just don't put your entire portfolio in junk bonds! Remember—diversify!

> ### Quick and Dirty Tip
>
> When considering investing in junk bonds, remember that junk bonds usually trade very similarly to an equity, like a stock, with respect to the returns you'll receive and the level of risk involved. In other words, just because they're called "bonds" doesn't mean they're necessarily safe, because different bonds have different flavors and colors and risk factors.

Bond Ratings

Because not all bonds are created equally, look at the type of bond and their ratings when you are considering investing in them. There are many ratings companies, such as Standard & Poor's, Moody's, and Fitch, that will have information on all the bonds that are available from a company or government. The three leading bond rating agencies, S&P, Moody's, and Fitch, rate bonds from the highest grade quality of AAA all the way to the lowest quality of C, though technically a bond could have a D rating for "default." A triple-A bond, AAA, would have a higher rating than a double-A bond, AA, which would have a higher rating than a single A bond, just as a triple-B bond (BBB) would have a higher rating than a double-B bond (BB) and so on all the way down to a single C. A rating of AAA is called prime, while a rating of C suggests high speculative risk and the possibility of default. The ratings are intended to tell you the relative safety of a bond and of the issuer; the higher the bond is rated, the less likely it is that the issuer of the bond will default. Technically, the ratings are a scale of potential for default. For example, U.S. bonds have the highest rating, a triple A rating; therefore, we don't worry about default, because we have the full taxing power of our country backing those bonds. In contrast, companies with triple C ratings have a greater potential for default.

Here's my bottom line on bonds: bonds are the safest of the four major investing vehicles, because you are virtually guaranteed to get back what you invested with interest. They provide stability and predictability, but in exchange, investors typically get smaller returns or profits.

Mutual Funds

As mentioned earlier, a mutual fund is a group of investments—like stocks and bonds—selected and managed by a money manager or group of money managers whose goal is to beat a benchmark index, such as the S&P 500. Because picking stocks and building your own portfolio can be difficult, a lot of investors trust money managers to do the choosing for them.

When you invest in a mutual fund, your money is pooled with other investors' money, which is then used to buy many types of stocks, bonds, or other investments. You don't own the actual stocks or bonds held in the mutual fund; rather you own a piece of the fund itself, in the form of shares. When the value of the underlying investments rises and falls, so does the value of your fund shares. You can only buy or sell shares of a mutual fund once a day—at the end of the business day. And in order to buy shares, you often have to call a broker or purchase funds from a particular company. In other words, you have to deal with a middleman. Because mutual funds are managed by individuals or teams, they often have high expense ratios, which means that you will be paying from 1 percent to 3 percent of your investment each year to the management team to select stocks that will hopefully outperform the market.

There are literally thousands of mutual funds to choose from. Online Web sites like Yahoo! Finance, Google Finance, and Morningstar can help you select a mutual fund. You can also speak with your financial advisor. I can't tell you which type to buy because my advice would depend on a number of factors, including your overall financial goals and how long you have to invest.

Here's my bottom line on mutual funds: mutual funds can be an easy way to have a diversified portfolio, but remember they come with relatively high management fees. Even if the fund you choose beats the market in a given year, it has to beat the market by more than the expense fees you are paying. If one year the S&P 500 returned 5 percent and your mutual fund returned 7 percent, but you had annual fees of 3 percent, your fund actually underperformed the S&P 500 by 1 percent. Some mutual funds beat the market or their benchmark by a very big margin, and so they are certainly worth the fee. Not all mutual funds will do this, however. So, make sure to find funds with low expense ratios that outperform.

Exchange Traded Funds (ETFs)

Because mutual funds often incur high management fees, I like investing in *exchange-traded funds* (ETFs). ETFs are basically mutual funds that can be bought and sold just like shares of stock of publicly held companies. Like mutual funds, ETFs invest in a basket of stocks and bonds (or other securities), but unlike mutual funds, they are bought and sold with fluctuating prices throughout the day, just like stocks on the stock exchanges. Unlike mutual funds, where a buy or sell order is filled only at the end of the trading day, the holdings of ETFs are constantly updated. ETFs don't need to be actively managed like mutual funds do, thus keeping the percentage of fund assets spent to operate the fund low—and much lower fees than that of mutual funds.

So how do ETFs work? Remember I mentioned the stock indexes, particularly the Dow and the S&P 500, in the section on stocks? Well, the largest and most well-known ETFs track, or mirror, these types of indexes, and therefore offer great diversification to investors.

The DIA and the Dow

Let's start with the symbol DIA, or the ETF better known as the "Diamonds." The DIA is an ETF that gives investment exposure to the thirty Dow Jones Industrial stocks. Before the days of ETFs, if you wanted to mirror the performance of the Dow Jones index, you would have to buy the thirty stocks or components of the index in the right balance. That would have been a difficult task, resulting in thirty separate commissions. That's no fun!

Now, through the DIA ETF, you can buy one investment that behaves just like an individual stock, which, in essence, is just like buying each of the thirty stocks in the Dow. The ETF managers balance their holdings to mirror the Dow Jones index as closely as possible. Most of the time, the DIA is one one-hundredth of the actual index, so, for example, if the Dow Jones index is at 10,000, the DIA would cost $100 to purchase one share of exposure. Owning that share would be just like owning one share approximately representing all thirty Dow Jones stock components—the quick and dirty way to buy the Dow.

Instead of paying a fee to a mutual fund manager to pick a handful of stocks to try to outperform a benchmark index, such as the Dow Jones, which might not happen, by purchasing a DIA ETF we seek to mirror the Dow Jones and return almost exactly what it returns.

The SPY and the S&P 500 Index

There are two other major U.S. stock-market ETFs. The largest and perhaps most well known might be the cool-sounding SPY fund. The SPY, often nicknamed the "Spiders," tracks the S&P

500 index, which you'll remember consists of 500 carefully selected stocks designed to be representative of the entire U.S. stock market. Though most investors often track the Dow Jones index, made up of only thirty stocks, others prefer to get a better feel of the stock market by looking at the S&P 500. The SPY ETF gives investors a way to get as close as possible to making a direct investment in the broad-based U.S. stock market.

The SPY fund is approximately one-tenth of what the S&P 500 index is quoting at a given moment. For example, if the S&P 500 is at 1,000, then the SPY ETF will cost you approximately $100 to purchase one share. That gives you virtually instant exposure to 500 stocks, and it's as if you just bought all 500 stocks in the S&P 500 in one transaction with one commission. That's a bargain! You would have to buy 500 stocks in perfect proportion to match the power and effectiveness of the SPY, and then pay commissions on all of those stocks. Until the SPY came along, doing that was almost impossible for retail investors. Now with the click of a button or by making a phone call, you can purchase 500 stocks with a single commission in a single fund. Remember that you're not actually purchasing the stocks, but mirroring the performance of the index through the ETF, which owns the stocks.

The QQQQs and the NASDAQ

Perhaps the third most popular ETF is the QQQQs, or "Quad Qs." Since this ETF invests in all of the stocks in the NASDAQ 100, investment in the ETF tracks that index. Again, the Quad Qs tracks the NASDAQ 100 index, which is comprised mostly of technology companies like Microsoft, Apple, Google, Intel, and Dell.

The Quad Qs are about one-fiftieth of the NASDAQ Index, or stated in easier-to-understand language, the NASDAQ 100 index is about 50 times the price value of the QQQQ. So, if the NASDAQ-100 is quoted at 2,000, then you can purchase one share of the QQQQs for about $40 to get broad-based exposure to all 100 stocks in the NASDAQ-100 index. This often makes it the cheapest of the three major-market ETFs, which gives it a certain appeal. Sometimes the SPY or DIA can seem too expensive for many investors, as they are often priced over $100 per share.

Where to Find More Information on ETFs

DIA, SPY, and QQQQs are the three most popular ETFs, and you can find plenty of information about them at Yahoo! Finance, Bloomberg, Google Finance, MSN Money, or any major Web site that details free information on stocks and exchange-traded funds. Just type in their symbols: DIA for the Dow Jones Diamonds, SPY for the S&P 500 Spiders, and QQQQ for the NASDAQ Quad Qs. Remember, you can purchase ETFs just like you would purchase a stock, using your online brokerage account or through your broker or money manager.

There are also ETFs beyond stock market–specific ETFs. ETFs can be used to gain exposure to other markets, including bonds, foreign countries, currencies, and commodities. Although it's too much to cover here, you should know there are over 600 ETFs out there—and the number grows each year. The quick and dirty tip is, don't invest in an ETF that trades less than 50,000 shares per day.

International Investments

International investing—investing in companies based in foreign countries—is another great way to diversify your portfolio. By including exposure to both domestic and foreign stocks in your portfolio, you'll reduce the risk that you'll lose money because international investment returns sometimes move in a different direction than U.S. market returns. Sure there are risks, but there are risks in the domestic market as well. Deciding how to invest is just a matter of doing the research and understanding the possibilities for the downside, then weighing those risks against your investment needs.

Why Consider International Investments?

Over the past thirty years, annual returns for the index that tracks the major international stock markets have done better than the domestic market in sixteen out of thirty years. Emerging markets—countries with rapid business growth as they move toward industrialization—can have double- or triple-digit returns in a year. Maybe more important is you also gain currency exposure. When the dollar drops, foreign investments are worth more for those U.S. dollar–based investors when they withdraw their funds, and vice versa.

One good way to invest internationally is through mutual funds that invest in foreign stocks.

+ **Global funds** invest primarily in foreign companies, though they may also invest in American companies.
+ **International funds** generally limit their investments to companies outside the United States.
+ **Regional or country funds** invest primarily in companies located in a specific geographical region (such as Asia) or in a single country. Some funds invest only in emerging markets, whereas others concentrate on more developed markets.
+ **International index funds** try to track the results of a particular foreign-market index.

Another way to invest internationally is through ETFs. As with mutual funds, there are region-specific and country-specific

ETFs. You can also invest in an ETF that tracks an international index. The two most popular international ETFs trade under the symbols EEM (iShares MSCI Emerging Markets fund) and EFA (iShares EAFE Index fund), which concentrate on investments in Europe, Australia, and the Far East (including Japan). For country-specific ETFs, you can use the iShares family funds, which include symbol EWJ for Japan, EWA for Australia, EWU for the United Kingdom, and other specific country ETFs. You can find more information at www.ishares.com.

Quick and Dirty Tip

If you are just starting to think about international investments, look to mutual funds. The variety of different mutual funds encompasses just about everything most investors should need. There are funds that specialize in stocks, in bonds, in bonds and stocks, and in money market funds.

Now you have the knowledge to deal with the basic investing vehicles: stocks, bonds, mutual funds, and ETFs. However, before you invest, you still have to undertake some research to make sure that the investments you choose are right for you. To do that, you need to overcome any fear you may have about investing, by determining your risk comfort levels.

3

Overcoming Investing Fear and What You Need to Know about Risk

And Other Emotions That May Be Getting in Your Way

One reason I wanted to write this book now is that many people are feeling that the whole world fell apart in 2008—or at least the whole *financial* world—and that investing will never be the same. So many people have asked me, "What can I do so I don't have to worry about my portfolio?" I call this the "sleep-at-night" problem. Since 2000 and more so since 2008, investors have become more acutely aware of—and more concerned about—their money, their investments, and their financial future in general. Almost everyone is anxious, and many people are downright fearful. In fact, fear is the biggest issue in any market environment: investors have a fear of losing as well as a fear of missing out if they *don't* do something.

You don't have to be scared of investing. In this chapter we'll take a look at common types of risk and then strategies for dealing with them. Hopefully I'll be able to allay some of your investing fear along the way.

How to Avoid the Risk of Massive Losses

Many investors ask me, "How can I make money with no risk?" That's the dream of many investors. Some people think it's possible because risk *can* be dissipated over time. Well, it can, and it can't.

If you look at a long enough time frame, there is very little risk in investing, because companies and stocks often recover, and the long-term trend of the stock market—or its historical movement—has clearly been up. For many, many years, the basic approach to investing was the Sleeping Beauty theory discussed in chapter 1: put your money into some investment and let it ride. You might have a couple of down years, but generally speaking, over time a chart depicting the value of your investments would have gone from the low on the bottom left to the high on the top right every time.

Unfortunately, that all changed because of the ferocity—and the velocity—and the extreme nature of the market moves starting in 2000. Since that intense movement of the stock market to the downside, and the essential obliteration of money, we are left with a situation that turns the idea of buy-and-hold on its head.

So how can you avoid risk? Well, actually you probably don't want to avoid risk; instead, you want to avoid the risk of massive loss. That's what investors really fear. The problem, of course, is that nobody knows where the next big drop-off is going to be.

There are two ways to minimize getting pummeled. First of all, you could take what's called a market neutral strategy, an approach to investing where you have a foot in and a foot out at the same time. You accomplish this by hedging.

Hedging

Hedging is a financial strategy used to reduce or minimize risk. Think of hedging like this: you put a hedge around something when you want to protect it, right? Taking an umbrella outside on a cloudy day is a way of "hedging" yourself against a rainstorm. You don't know that it's going to rain, but if it does, then the extra burden of carrying the umbrella will be worth it. When you hear someone say you should "hedge your portfolio," think of the word *hedge* as the word *protection*. By hedging, we try to protect our carefully selected portfolio against the uncertainty of the future. Hedges are not free, however. In the umbrella example, if it didn't rain, then you would have carried the extra weight of the umbrella around all day.

What hedging means is that you're not going to benefit from all of the upsides of the markets but you're also not going to suffer all of the downs either. It is very difficult to come back from a devastating market loss, so we need to find a way to offset losses in a time of a market downturn. There are specific ETFs you can use when you want to hedge your portfolio for a period of time. We buy stocks now because we believe the price will increase in the future. However, if we believe there will be a temporary period of weakness ahead in the market and we do not feel like we should sell our entire portfolio, we might choose to put on a temporary hedge for a period of time. Another reason to hedge instead of selling off your portfolio is that you get the benefit of reduced taxes if you hold stocks longer than a year.

There are two main ways investors can hedge their portfolio. First, they can purchase an inverse exchange-traded fund. An inverse ETF gains value as the market goes down because it is structured to make money when stocks decline. An investor can choose to purchase shares of an inverse index ETF such as the SH, which is the ProShares Short S&P 500 Fund (it is the inverse counterpart of the SPY).

In the event that the S&P 500 declines, the SH fund will increase in value while the SPY or stocks in your portfolio will decline. The SH is the umbrella protecting your portfolio from the downside of the market. When you feel the rain is over and determine that the market will start rising again, then you sell your shares of the SH (or other inverse ETF), and perhaps you make a profit on this short-term hedge. During the time you have the hedge on your portfolio, the inverse position made money while your broader portfolio declined. When you take off the hedge, or sell your shares, you sell the hedge at a profit (let's say $5,000), but now your portfolio has declined by $5,000 during the sell-off. Had you not put on the hedge, you would have a portfolio down $5,000, but because you put on the hedge—even though your portfolio still declined $5,000—you have a profit of $5,000 that offsets the loss. If you were correct that this was just a temporary decline in the market, then the value of your portfolio should continue to rise.

If you were wrong and the market continued to rise after you put on the hedge, you would lose the $5,000 because the value of your hedge, the inverse ETF, would have declined. However, the price of your portfolio would have increased by $5,000, so again you would be back where you started before putting on the hedge. You can choose to hedge a percentage of your portfolio (say 25 percent or 50 percent), or you can hedge your full portfolio.

The other method of hedging your portfolio involves buying put options, which are like tiny insurance contracts on individual stocks in your portfolio. If you buy a put, the put option will rise in value as your stock declines. However, if you buy a put option and the prices of your stocks continue to rise, you only lose the money you paid to purchase the put option (just like the hassle of carrying the umbrella).

Read carefully about buying puts or inverse index ETFs before doing so. There are a lot of little caveats that you need to know before investing.

Have a Diversified Portfolio

The second major way to help minimize your chances of massive loss is to have a truly diversified portfolio. In the past, a diversified portfolio meant you had invested in perhaps ten or fifteen different mutual funds in different sectors and different countries. But in 2007–2008, that type of diversification didn't really work. If you invested only in stocks—whether individual stocks, mutual funds, and/or ETFs—then you weren't sufficiently diversified because your whole portfolio lost value. You could have been invested in the United States, Africa, Europe, or China; it didn't matter where you invested in equities, because everything fell and you got hurt. However, if you had true diversification—that is, if you were invested in stocks, bonds, and real estate—then even though your investments in stocks and real estate lost significant value, your bonds did much better (even though their interest rates came down sharply).

Different Types of Risk

Though most people focus on the loss of money when thinking about risk, there are actually many other types of risk that you'll want to minimize as well. One of these is the risk of inflation, an interesting type of risk that can create a serious situation for many investors because it's ever present, yet invisible to most.

Inflation Risk

Inflation risk is the risk of the purchasing power of the dollar diminishing over time. For example, if you have $10,000 and put it under your mattress, then twenty-five years from now, if you take it out, it's going to be worth less than it is today. That is simply because a loaf of bread or a gallon of milk or anything else you want to buy is going to cost much more in twenty-five years. Though it may cost $1 for a loaf of bread today, at some time in the future, that same loaf of bread may cost $20. In the 1940s, it cost around 10 cents to see a movie in a theater. Now, you're lucky to buy a movie ticket for under $10! So if things cost more twenty-five years from now, that means the buying power of the cash under your mattress will go down. Your purchasing power will diminish as the years go on because other things will become more expensive. That might not happen in a year or two, but eventually your $10,000 will be worth much less than when you stuffed it under your mattress.

What can you do to limit the negative effects of inflation risk? Well, instead of stashing your money under the mattress or keeping it in cash, you could buy CDs (certificates of deposit), which require you to deposit your funds with a bank for a stated period of time. During the time period, or term, your money earns interest based upon an agreed method of calculating the rate. Because you earn interest on your CDs, the amount you invest will grow as the years go on. CDs can protect against inflation, but it's not guaranteed. If you're receiving only a 3 percent interest rate on your CD, and inflation happens to be 3 percent as well, then after you've paid taxes on the interest, you'll actually be losing money on your original investment. But that would still be better than leaving your money under your mattress.

Inflation risk is insidious because you don't see it. It's like you're going down the road in the car, and there's a *little* hole in your gas tank. You don't notice you're losing gas until you run out of gas, but once that happens, you definitely have a problem.

What can you do? You should consider several alternative investments in addition to CDs to counter the effect of inflation. You can be partially invested in the stock market, because stocks tend to outpace inflation, under most circumstances. You should also consider investing in Treasury Inflation-Protected Securities

(TIPS). TIPS are bonds issued by the U.S. government that pay interest every six months and pay the principal—the original amount you invested—when the bond matures. An additional benefit is that the coupon payments and underlying principal are increased to compensate for inflation, as measured by the consumer price index (CPI). The downside to investing in TIPS is that they may pay a low rate of return, but that's the price you pay for protecting your money from the ravages of inflation risk! Inflation risk helps to show why it's a smart idea to have some money in the stock market, even though it's a riskier investment because your money isn't guaranteed as it is with bonds. Now are you starting to see why everyone talks about diversification?

You might also consider investing in precious metals, such as gold or silver, or even in commodities, which are basic goods, such as many food items (e.g., soybeans, corn), oil, and other products that are undifferentiated among brands. (A more complete discussion of commodities is provided in chapter 10.) Commodities can also help protect your portfolio from inflation risk because when inflation occurs, there is a cost-of-living adjustment; the cost of living is made up of the cost of goods, and those goods are commodities. Because the price of commodities rises with inflation, investing in commodities means you should make money on them.

To mitigate the effects of inflation, you need to keep up to date on the current rate of inflation. There are several places you can find information regarding the CPI, including:

+ www.bls.gov (Bureau of Labor Statistics)
+ www.inflationdata.com
+ www.stlouisfed.org (St. Louis Federal Reserve)

If you go to www.bls.gov, you'll find a CPI inflation calculator (enter "inflation calculator" in the keyword box), which allows you to calculate the difference in any amount for any two years. For example, $1 in 1980 had the same buying power as $2.65 in 2010.

Knowing the current inflation rate is important because your investments need to do better than the inflation rate. For example, in a deflationary environment, any investment you have just has to do better than stay flat. Even if it's earning only 1 percent, it's doing better than the inflation rate.

Of course, no one knows what the inflation rate is going to be in the future. What you need to do is look at your inflation-adjusted rate of return of your investments, which is also known as the *real rate of return*. For example, if you earn 5 percent on your investments and if inflation is 2 percent, then your *real rate of return* is 3 percent (before taxes).

Reinvestment Risk

In addition to the risks of inflation and the loss of principal, you also need to know about *reinvestment risk*. Let's use our earlier example and say you invest in a CD paying a 3 percent interest rate. Suppose that the interest you're earning on your CD flows into your money market account or savings account on an annual or semiannual basis. You don't want to keep that new income in your savings or money market account because it won't grow enough in there. So when that happens, you have to make a decision: where do you reinvest that money? If interest rates go down and you do keep the money in either of those accounts, then you're reinvesting at a *lower* interest rate than your original 3 percent. If you can't reinvest your money into another investment that earns a comparable level of interest and that will keep pace with your goals, then you're going to lose out on income opportunities. So what you need to do is make sure you find alternative investments for that money.

The Risk of Default

In addition to the three types of risk we've discussed, there's also the *risk of default*. Recall that chapter 2 described a few of the various types of bonds: U.S. Treasury bonds, corporate bonds, municipal bonds, and junk bonds. With some types of bonds, there is greater risk of default.

For example, suppose you invest in corporate bonds from Company ABC. Then you find out that Company ABC is not doing so well financially. Maybe there's a lawsuit against the company, or maybe it's potentially going bankrupt. Whatever the reason, Company ABC is going to be defaulting on its bonds and not paying off its bondholders—including you.

That's why, when you consider investing in bonds as we discussed in the previous chapter, you should look at the ratings from the various ratings services. Make sure you understand there is a risk, even though those bonds are backed by a company that may seem sound at the time. Treasury bonds, which are backed by the full faith and credit of the U.S. government, are considered one of the safest investments because they are supported by the full taxing power of the government. You don't have that level of guarantee with a corporate bond. So the quick and dirty tip for avoiding risk from default is to make smart bond purchases from the get-go. Buy quality bonds only, and consider insurance on municipal bonds if you prefer the safer route.

Opportunity Risk

Another type of risk you need to minimize is *opportunity risk* or, more precisely, lost opportunity risk. This is the risk you face when you have money but you don't invest it in anything. In that case, you're not gaining anything from the use of your money, because you're just letting it sit. Of course, you may decide that's what you want to do, because you may want to have cash on hand to use at any time, without having to worry about it not being available when you need it. In this case you don't risk losing any of that money except to inflation risk, which can be significant. If you don't invest your $10,000, you won't risk losing any part of it, but if you're not investing, you have no potential for gain. And in order to save enough for retirement or pay for their children's education, most people need their money to grow.

Lost opportunity risk is not so easy to quantify. Many investors think, "I could have made a killing if only I'd invested in X." For example, my firm invested in AOL stock in the very early days, but it was really just serendipitous that we found out about it. One night I was at a hockey game, and the guys sitting behind me were talking about AOL the whole time. Now this was years before AOL was a household name, and their talk got my attention. When I went back to the office, I researched the company and decided we should invest in it. This happened only because I happened to be sitting in that seat in front of those guys, and that was my opportunity.

What if I had heard that conversation but not done anything about it? That's how the risk of lost opportunities comes into play. You can't expect to go to a hockey game and just happen to pick up an investing tidbit. You need to keep your eyes open and to manage your money as actively as you can. (I'll discuss identifying good investment opportunities in chapter 4.)

Liquidity Risk

Another type of interesting risk is *liquidity risk*. How easily can you buy or sell an investment? For example, let's say you need money to pay for an unexpected medical bill so you decide to sell some stock. If no one wants to buy your shares and you can't convert them to cash, it means your investment isn't liquid. Small-cap stocks (stocks in companies valued under $1 billion) and especially micro-cap stocks (less than $250 in market capitalization) are less liquid because there is often a limited and smaller market for small caps, and it may be a little bit harder to sell them.

On the other hand, investors trade large-cap stocks (companies usually valued at more than $5 billion), such as IBM (IBM) or Microsoft (MSFT) or Exxon Mobil (XOM), all the time. Often millions of shares are traded per day, so there's not much liquidity risk with these investments.

Liquidity risk doesn't pertain only to the stock market, of course. There's also liquidity risk in CDs, bonds, annuities, or other investments that require you to hold on to it for a period of time without incurring a penalty to sell. Of course, liquidity risk is often worthwhile, because the investment you're buying (such as a CD) offers you guarantees regarding the interest that you'll earn on your money as well as the principal. Taking that risk may be okay with you, but you still need to understand liquidity risk—that you might not be able to turn your investment into cash exactly when you need it—before you invest $1 in anything.

Tax Risk

Tax risks depend on the type of investment you have, so you have to evaluate your investments on an apples-to-apples basis. For example, suppose you have invested in two mutual funds. Although both of them may grow 15 percent in one year, one of them may generate more income to you, because it pays dividends and capital gains. Capital gains are the increase in the value of a stock or investment that the mutual fund sold in a given year. Remember that mutual funds buy and sell stocks and if they have high turnover rates (if they buy and sell a lot of stocks in a year), then they likely will have higher capital gain distributions. However, that means you, the shareholder, have to pay taxes on these benefits! Funds usually distribute these payments to shareholders at the end of the year. Shareholders are required to pay taxes on them the year they are received, even though most of the time these benefits are reinvested. When you make money on your investments, you need to pay taxes on it, of course. Thus, the net income you gain in a year on a mutual fund may be lower than the net income you gain on the other mutual fund that didn't pay out any interest, dividends, or capital gains distributions in that calendar year. Therefore, you have to look at the *net after-tax return* on your investments in order to make an accurate comparison of how your mutual fund investments are performing.

Note: This is *not* the same as when you *lose* 10 percent of your investment—for example, where you had $100,000 invested in something, and you lost 10 percent, so now you have $90,000. Many investors don't take into consideration the tax risk (or other types of risk) because the only thing that many investors focus on, calculate, and quantify is the potential loss of their *principal*, because it is more visible.

The Bottom Line

Minimizing risk should be a big factor in your investment choices. You have to decide the balance between risk and reward. You'll always have to balance gaining money and protecting money over your lifetime. If you don't take any risk at all, preferring to stash your cash in your mattress, you'll lose over time as inflation causes the price of everything to go up except the money you've hidden away. However, if you take too much risk, maybe by buying the wrong junk bonds or putting your entire portfolio into a single micro-cap stock, then you could lose all or most of your portfolio in a short period of time. You have to find a personal balance between fear of loss and unbridled greed.

If you are younger, you can usually take more risk because you can weather the volatility and offset any losses with the salary you earn over the years. You can also hold through rough times in the economy and take on slightly more risk because you want your portfolio to grow over a long period of time. However, if you are near retirement, you won't have as much flexibility or ability to bounce back if you suffer losses in your portfolio. In retirement, you're much more worried about keeping what you have safe instead of growing your portfolio with high-risk investments. You're better off concentrating in bonds and low-risk, blue-chip, large-cap stocks that pay solid dividends. Therefore your need to balance risk changes over the course of your investing lifetime.

You'll still need to have a diversified portfolio of different types of bonds; small-cap, mid-cap, large-cap, growth, and value stocks; international funds; and other broader investment vehicles such as mutual funds and exchange-traded funds. Now, with the world of ETFs open to you, you can easily diversify your portfolio into sectors, commodities, currencies, index funds, and so much more. Diversification is a type of protection that will help calm your fears as you make your investment decisions over time.

Don't put all your investing eggs in one basket, or in one stock. Don't be afraid to sell an investment that is underperforming or no longer meets your criterion for inclusion in your portfolio. For example, you might have a rule that you will sell any investment that declines 10 percent from the price at which you purchased it. This may sound arbitrary, but imagine how much money you could save yourself if you sold stocks that were down 10 percent or 15 percent that later continued their decline by 50 percent or more! That would have been a good rule to follow during both the 2001 and 2008 bear markets in stocks. Many technology stocks fell over 80 percent from 2000 to 2003, while many financial stocks fell over 80 percent from 2007 to 2009. Selling an underperforming investment is a type of protection that can save you from larger losses in the future. We all get so caught up in what hot stock or sector to buy, that we often don't spend enough time thinking about when to take profits or trim our portfolio of declining investments, just like we would clear our flower garden of weeds and dead blossoms. Don't fall in love with your stock purchases either, or you will find it difficult to sell it when you need to.

Now that you know something about the various risks you need to consider, let's take a look at key trends you should track so that you can decide *what* you may want to invest in.

4

Key Trends You Should Track— and How to Get Ideas for What to Invest In

Unemployment, Shopping, Real Estate and the Housing Market, Construction, Materials, Manufacturing, and More

Now that you know something about how to invest and the risks you need to consider, let's take a look at how you can find ideas for what to invest in. In the old days, people used to brag about getting "a hot stock tip," but today there's so much information available in newspapers and magazines, and on TV and the Internet that we're inundated with possibilities. As mentioned in chapter 1, we are in a world plagued with information overload. Though it's true that the media typically provides recommendations on what looks good and what doesn't, I prefer to watch certain economic indicators instead because they give us clues into what's happening in the economy—which in turn helps us decide what to invest in.

In this chapter I'll tell you what indicators are, which ones to look out for, what they tell you about the economy, and how you can then use this information to make smarter investment decisions.

What Are Indicators and Why Should I Pay Attention?

Indicators are basically pieces of information that provide a bird's-eye view into the state of the economy. The whole point of looking at indicators is to get clues. Why are these clues so important? Because it can be very tricky to understand the economy and to know if we're in a recession, about to be in a recession, in recovery, and so on. Entire college and graduate classes are devoted to explaining the economy, and you can find innumerable books on the topic—but this book isn't one of them. Instead I'm going to give you the quick and dirty version of what you need to know so that you can go out and make better investment decisions.

Understanding the Economy

To understand the economy, you need to know how it's measured. You can measure a local economy—that of a particular state, for example—but when I'm talking about the economy, I mean the economy of the United States as a whole. One way to measure that is by looking at the gross domestic product, or GDP.

The GDP

The *gross domestic product (GDP)* of the United States measures the value of the economic activity that's going on. Basically, it's the monetary value of all the goods and services the country produces during a specific period of time. There are other, more complicated ways to measure the economy, but the GDP is one of the most basic calculations that gives us a global view of the economy as a whole. The simplest formula economists use to calculate the GDP is to add up all private consumption, total investment, and government spending, and then to add or subtract the difference between what the United States is exporting and what it's importing.

The government releases this all-important number once each quarter (every three months), generally in the final week of the quarter. You'll hear all about the GDP from the financial media and in the economic section of any major newspaper or financial Web site. It is a very important number, and it's hard to miss.

To have a healthy economy, the GDP should increase each quarter. If the GDP is negative, it could be a sign that the economy is slipping toward a recession. In fact, economists often define a recession as two consecutive quarters—that's six months—of negative GDP growth.

The GDP number is released as a percentage, which is calculated on an annualized basis—that is, it projects what the GDP would be for the whole year based on the information they have when the figure is released. This is why you sometimes hear television commentators say, "The economy grew at a 3 percent annualized rate of growth," when referring to the GDP.

Different Sectors of the Economy

An economy is made up of many different sectors, which can also be measured. Some of the main sectors of the U.S. economy include manufacturing, retail, real estate, health care, and energy, but there are many others as well. You don't need to know all the different measures; you just need to know that there are a number of different sectors you can invest in.

How do you know which sector to invest in? As we've said, indicators can give us a clue about the state of the economy as a whole, as well as about how certain sectors are doing. This is helpful when it comes to deciding how to invest your money.

The Economic Cycle

Now you know some basic information about the economy. The next important thing to know is that the economy moves in cycles: an economy is not always up or down but changes continuously.

The four stages of the economic, or business, cycle are:

+ **Growth**: Also known as expansion, growth is when the pace of economic activity speeds up.
+ **Peak**: The point when economic activity is the highest, also known as a top.
+ **Contraction**: The point when economic activity starts to slow down. If a contraction is severe enough, it may signal a recession.
+ **Trough**: The point when economic activity is at its lowest, also known as a bottom.

Figure 1 illustrates the economic cycle from peak to trough. The best way to understand Figure 1 is to start in the middle on

Figure 1. The Economic Cycle: From Peak to Trough

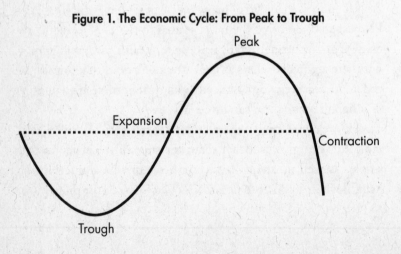

the left and move forward to the right, taking in account the different curves of the chart. The curved line shows what phase the economy is in as we move forward in time. As shown in the example, the economy, from left to right, moves forward from trough (bottom), to expansion, to peak (top) to contraction, and back to an eventual trough that gives way to another expansion. (Note that if the contraction is steep enough, it is labeled a recession.)

Now look at the dotted line that cuts the curved line in half in the middle. This dotted line is the zero growth line, or zero line. Stated simply, when the curved line representing the economy is above the straight line (zero line), then the economy is in a growth phase, expanding with a positive GDP growth. When the curved line (economy) is under the straight zero line, then the economy is in contraction or recession (negative GDP growth). It is possible for the economy to contract, or slow, the rate of growth without traveling under the zero growth line, which would mean that the GDP slowed, but did not turn negative. An economy is said to be in recession when GDP growth remains negative.

Expansion and Contraction

In Figure 1, the horizontal "zero" line separates the economy into two main phases: *expansion* and *contraction*. Remember that an economy has to peak before it heads into a recession, and the economy does not magically fall into a recession one evening. It takes a while for economic conditions to deteriorate, which is indicated by the curved line falling but still being above the zero line. When the economy is moving downward but is still above the zero line, it means we're growing less fast and are probably on the way to a contraction phase. If the contraction phase we move into is deep enough, it becomes a recession. A number of indicators will tell us that the economy is declining and that we should be prepared for a contraction—and a possible recession.

Similarly, when the economy bottoms (forms a trough) and begins rising, it first must go through a phase of indicators improving, or getting less bad. Maybe last quarter the GDP was −3 percent, but this quarter it is −1.5 percent. We're still in a contraction phase because the GDP is negative, but the bad numbers are not as bad and are getting better. Thus we may expect the economy will soon turn the corner to the positive side and enter an expansion phase. The purpose of watching the indicators is to get an idea of where we are moving in the economic cycle. For example, we might know we're in an expansion phase, but certain indicators will tell us we're growing less fast, which may indicate we're possibly transitioning into a new part of the economic cycle. For a clearer picture of the cycle, view the stock-market charts in chapter 5 that discuss trends in the stock market. They show how a market, which reflects the health or weakness of the broader economy, goes through cycles similar to what I've just described.

Why is paying attention to where we are in the cycle important? It's because it should influence your investing decisions. If the economy is in the growth, or expansion cycle, you'll want to do certain things that you would never do if the economy were in the contraction, or recession, cycle. For example, during a strong economic expansion, you should probably invest more in the stock market and less in conservative investments like bonds or cash. However, during a steep contraction phase, your portfolio should be more concentrated in safer assets like bonds and cash. It's like the difference in playing offense or defense in football. When you have the ball (when the economy is in a strong expansion phase), your goal is to score as many points—or make as much money through investing—as possible. When you are on defense and do not have the ball (when the economy is contracting sharply), your goal is to prevent the other team from scoring. In our analogy this means protecting the money you have and losing as little as possible.

So how can we tell where we are in the cycle? You guessed it—indicators. Because there's no set amount of time the economy spends in each phase of the cycle, it can be hard to tell when we are moving to a new phase. It's not as though the economy changes phases every six months so that you know exactly when it'll be shifting. Figuring out what phase the economy is in isn't always easy; even economists differ on what the economy is doing and where it is moving at any given time. But I'm going to tell you which indicators I believe are the best at offering accurate clues about the economy so you'll be better equipped to make smart investing decisions.

The Three Types of Indicators

There are three main types of indicators:

+ Lagging indicators
+ Leading indicators
+ Coincident indicators

Following is the quick and dirty explanation of each.

Lagging Indicators

Lagging indicators are those that change after the economy has already begun to follow a particular trend in a cycle. For example, suppose in April the economy starts trending, or moving, from the trough stage to the growth stage. A lagging indicator wouldn't reflect we're in the growth stage until months later—maybe in July. Unemployment is an example of a lagging indicator because unemployment numbers don't start to change until after the economy is already in a new stage, or trend. When the economy starts to pick up, it still takes a while for unemployment levels to drop; when the economy starts to fall, it takes a while for unemployment levels to rise. Even though lagging indicators occur after the economic trend has started, they still can be very useful to investors because they can confirm you're in a particular place in the economic cycle. They also provide a better understanding of what's happening to the economy as a whole, and the more knowledge you have about the economy in general, the more you should be able to develop ideas for what you want to invest in.

Leading Indicators

A *leading indicator* is essentially the opposite of a lagging indicator; instead of following the economic trend, it precedes it. Leading indicators give you an indication of what is going to potentially happen in the future. The word *potentially* is important because we can never be sure about what's going to occur in the future; we can only consider what could happen and what might happen. Consumer confidence—how investors say they feel about the broader economy and their likelihood to spend money or save it—is an example of a leading indicator because it attempts to predict the future behavior of consumers. I'll discuss this more in a bit.

Coincident Indicators

The third type of general indicator is a *coincident indicator*. A coincident indicator moves in conjunction with the economy, and so these indicators show what's really transpiring, right now. Industrial production is a coincident indicator, because it directly correlates with the state of the economy. When the economy rises, industrial production rises; when the economy falls, industrial production falls. The same is true in retail sales; if the economy is rising, retail sales numbers are rising, and if the economy is falling, then retail sales numbers are falling. Think of coincident indicators as showing the level of activity the economy is experiencing now.

Which Indicators Should You Watch and Why?

Which indicators should you track? There are all kinds of specific indicators you should look at. I'm just going to give you the quick and dirty guide to the indicators I consider the most important.

A Word of Caution

It's important to pay attention to a range of different indicators before you make any investment decision. Using one indicator as a directive to sell a stock or invest in a particular ETF is dangerous, because one indicator doesn't give a complete view of the economy. You need to monitor a number of different indicators. When several signal the same thing, that's when you'll have the best sense about the state of the economy. This book is intended to give you a good idea of what information you should seek out, as well as to assist you in planning your investments more knowledgeably. It is not intended to be a cookbook, telling you to simply mix together various ingredients and make a million dollars. You shouldn't only be using this inexpensive book (or any other!) to invest your $100,000 portfolio—or even your $1,000 portfolio. Instead, you should view each indicator as part of the whole picture, or a piece of a big puzzle. Each individual indicator may be like a light bulb going off; each one gives you more evidence and that guides you to seek out more about other parts of the economy. Always consider all of the pieces of the big picture before you make any investing decision.

Unemployment Indicators

One major indicator you'll frequently hear the talking heads on TV discuss is the rate of unemployment. As mentioned earlier, unemployment figures are lagging indicators, so it's not going to indicate a possible change in the economic cycle—like consumer confidence might—but it might confirm that the cycle is in fact rising or falling. Reports on unemployment reveal a host of useful information for investors, and several will give you the overall jobs picture. You should look, on a regular basis, at the following:

+ **Initial unemployment claims**, which measures the number of individuals seeking state unemployment benefits for the first time, often after being laid off from a job. This number is released each Thursday morning by the Department of Labor. It is a volatile number, so economists often look at the four-week moving average of claims as well.
+ **Continuing claims** measures workers already receiving unemployment benefits. To be counted, a person must have previously been covered by unemployment insurance and be currently receiving benefits. This number is also released weekly by the Department of Labor.
+ **Total number of unemployed people**, which measures all unemployed people, whether or not they receive unemployment benefits. Initial claims and continuing claims reports count only those individuals who are receiving unemployment benefits; they do not include the people who have fallen off the rolls because they have exceeded the maxi-

mum number of months for unemployment insurance. Because individuals cannot receive unemployment benefits forever, if they have not found a job by the time their benefits expire, they are not counted in standard government reports. This number can be difficult for economists to calculate accurately, but it gives a truer sense of the unemployed situation in the country.

You can track these and other unemployment statistics on the following Web sites:

+ www.briefing.com
+ www.economy.com
+ www.dismal.com
+ www.bls.gov, the Bureau of Labor Statistics online
+ www.stlouisfed.org, the Web site of the St. Louis Reserve Bank

The direct link for weekly unemployment reports each Thursday morning that track initial and continuing claims is on the Department of Labor Web site: www.dol.gov/opa/media/press/eta/main.htm.

Most leading economic Web sites not only release the official number, but also include a chart of the last few months or years of data, which is often more important to investors than the current unemployment figure. One of the best Web sites for tracking current and past changes in the unemployment report is from Econoday via Bloomberg at www.bloomberg.econoday.com. The Econoday Web site shows a list of major economic reports scheduled for the week, and you can see the analyst expectations, current numbers, and past trends by clicking on the name of the report in the calendar. To find the data on jobless claims, click on the report entitled "Jobless Claims," which is released every Thursday morning. The Web site provides a chart of the data for the last two years, with a four-week moving average (to smooth out the volatility) and provide a clearer picture of the trend in unemployment.

Jobs Report

You might also take a look at the jobs report (also called the non-farm payroll number), which the government releases on the first Friday of every month. It gives us a sense of whether we're gaining or losing jobs in the economy and the overall picture of employment. We can also look at the rate of job growth or loss by comparing this month's numbers to those of previous months.

The jobs report is actually two surveys combined into a single report. The first, the household survey, surveys 60,000 households, and the second, the establishment survey, surveys 400,000 worksites and businesses. Businesses report how many workers they currently have on their payrolls, how many hours these employees worked, and what their average hourly earnings are.

The Jobs Report also contains information on the average workweek, or how many hours on average the employees worked. The average workweek is viewed as a leading indicator for future employment numbers. Companies will cut hours for employees before laying them off during a downturn, and will increase the hours of current employees (even making some work overtime) before they decide to hire new employees during an economic expansion.

Beyond showing how many people gained or lost employment last month, the Jobs Report also tells you about the hourly workweek and average hourly earnings. A rising average workweek is generally considered a positive sign, as are rising average wages per week. These rising numbers indicate the health of the economy.

After all, if lots of people are employed and the economy is expanding, they're going to spend more money, which should give a boost to the economy. So paying attention to this report can tell you about the strength of the economy. In fact, some economists consider the Jobs Report to be one of the most important reports to watch in order to get a sense of broad economic activity. The key is to look deeper than just the headline unemployment rate number, which you're sure to find out quickly from the financial media. The headline number is actually a lagging indicator, while some of the deeper components, like hours worked, are seen as leading indicators. The headline number does not tell the full story, so be sure to look at the trends of the other components in the very important Jobs Report at the start of each month when it is released.

The Winning Investor's Strategy

Let's look at how you might use unemployment trends to help you make your investment decisions. When unemployment is rising, you might consider investing in job-hunting businesses—those companies that help people find jobs, like Monster.com (MWW) or Robert Half (RHI). If unemployment is starting to trend lower, these job-search businesses should be doing better, so you might consider investing in them. When you look at unemployment numbers, you have to do so in coordination with retail and consumer trends, like consumer confidence, which I'll discuss in a bit. That will help you discern which particular consumer-related stocks are going to have the biggest drag or benefit. For example, if consumer confidence is unchanged, but unemployment is rising, you might consider investing in businesses that sell everyday items at a discount, such as Walmart (WMT) and Target (TGT), instead of higher-priced stores and businesses that make or sell luxury items, such as Tiffany (TIF), Saks (SKS), and Nordstrom (JWN).

Quick and Dirty Lesson From the Market

Tracking unemployment indicators closely can clue you in to when certain sectors and companies are poised to do better. In 2009, my company was closely tracking unemployment trends and saw that it was finally starting to level off after having after risen dramatically over the previous months. That told us more people were going back to work and gave us the idea to invest in a company that would seemingly benefit from more people working. So we looked at Cintas (CTAS), which makes uniforms and other supplies (for example, for janitors and service people), because this company's business is directly linked to unemployment levels. Obviously, if fewer people are working, there's less demand for uniforms, and vice versa. When unemployment started to level off, we bought some Cintas stock, and profited about 22 percent over 3 months on that investment. That's an example of why you need to watch economic indicators—to give you winning ideas of where to invest.

If you've been tracking unemployment numbers, you'll notice when unemployment starts peaking and starts leveling off and then when it eventually starts to drop back down. When that occurs you can be somewhat assured we are moving into a period of economic expansion. This is because companies hire workers in response to rising demand and consumer spending across the economy. In a transition from a contraction to an expansion, employment numbers are one of the last major indicators to turn up. Again, they're lagging indicators. Companies will usually wait as long as possible before they hire new workers (choosing to make the ones they have work harder or longer) or fire long-time employees (especially in small businesses). Businesses take employment decisions very seriously. So if you're seeing strength in some other indicators we'll discuss in this chapter, such as consumer sentiment, retail sales, higher industrial production, and capacity utilization, and if you're also seeing drops in initial claims for unemployment insurance and a decline in the unemployment rate, it is often an all-clear sign to begin or continue investing strongly in leading stocks for your portfolio. You're on offense! Time to score!

Consumer Confidence

As mentioned, *consumer confidence* is a leading indicator, and so it is an economic measure that precedes a trend and can give us useful information about the future of the economy. To find out the consumer confidence number, the Conference Board surveys five thousand consumers each month on their attitude toward both present economic conditions and the future of the economy. They also ask consumers how willing they are to spend money. You can find the most recent data on the Conference Board Web site at www.conference-board.org/economics/ConsumerConfidence .cfm.

The consumer confidence number is released during the last week of the month, and, as with the GDP, you should be able to find it in the economic section of any major newspaper or on a financial Web site. If this month's number is higher than last month's, it indicates that consumers feel better about the economy and are much more likely to spend money, which drives the economy higher. More consumer spending translates into higher profits for companies, which often leads to higher stock prices. If the consumer confidence number is lower, however, it could be a sign that consumers are going to be saving their money instead of spending it, which translates into lower potential profits for companies and then lower stock prices. Investors watch this number very closely because consumer spending makes up a whopping two-thirds of the GDP number, which of course tells us the health of the economy as a whole.

The easiest way to understand the reasons for measuring and paying attention to consumer confidence is to know that if consumers feel confident, they are more likely to spend money than if they do not feel confident. When consumers spend money freely and are confident about the future of the economy, then retail sales increase and the economy expands. If consumers feel pessimistic about the economy, especially when unemployment is high and the media keep talking about bad economic conditions and a recession, then consumers are less likely to spend their hard-earned money, which does not paint a rosy picture for the future of the economy.

The Winning Investor's Strategy

Consumer confidence is not just a good sign about the overall economy, it's also a good signal for certain sectors of the economy, like retail. As I mentioned, when consumer confidence is up, people are more likely to spend money. So if you see that consumer confidence is starting to move up dramatically, you might consider investing in the retail sector or retail stocks. You might also take notice of the manufacturing sector (I'll tell you how to do this a little later) to research which manufacturing industries are on the rise. Then you can figure out what people may actually be buying—and thus get further insight into what to invest in. If furniture factories are getting busier, for example, you think about investing in companies like Furniture Brands (FBN) or Leggett & Platt (LEG) within the furniture industry.

Another idea is to consider investing in restaurant stocks because they also reflect consumer confidence. Obviously, people go out to eat less when they're watching their spending, especially when it comes to the more expensive restaurants. They pass up the $10 hamburger at sit-down restaurants in favor of $2 fast-food hamburgers. But that changes when consumer confidence rises. Once you decide you want to invest in retail stocks or restaurant stocks, you'll need to then figure out which retail or restaurant stocks are the best choices. In the future chapters on analysis, I'll help you do just that. We're tracking the indicators as a way to get winning ideas for the sectors we want to invest in, and then analysis will help us pick the best investments within those sectors.

Consumer confidence levels can also tell us what we *don't* want to invest in. If consumer confidence is falling, we're likely going to see lower levels of buying in the retail sector. When that happens, consider staying away from certain sectors of the stock market, like retail stocks. Staying away from retail stocks can mean not adding new retail stocks to your portfolio, but it can also mean taking steps to protect your portfolio from big losses. Aside from selling some or all of your retail stocks, you should also consider putting in protective *sell stops*, which are orders to sell a stock once the stock reaches a specified price. Let's say you think consumer confidence indicates the retail sector is going to start doing badly, but it hasn't yet. You don't want to sell all of your stock in The Gap (GPS), for example, because there's no guarantee that retail stocks will fall. But just in case you're right, you can decide that if the price of The Gap stock falls to a certain level, you will automatically sell it. So if that stock does in fact decline and continues to decline, then you have some protection in your portfolio from losing even more money. We'll talk more about sell stops in chapter 5.

As I mentioned, consumer confidence can give you insights into the future on consumer spending, which translates directly into retail sales. Consumer confidence and retail sales are not 100 percent correlated, because a survey respondent can say one thing (like they are feeling confident) and then do another (like save money). However, watching consumer confidence numbers can clue you in to the mind of consumers, and thus their behavior.

Quick and Dirty Tip

The first industry group to recover after a contraction is frequently retail, also known as the consumer discretionary sector. Often, the next two sectors to improve are materials and industrials (companies that make the products consumers buy). When consumers start spending after an economic contraction or recession, demand for goods pushes businesses to produce more products for the consumers to buy. That means that inventories need to be rebuilt, which often leads to a spike in manufacturing. Also, materials companies—businesses that turn raw materials into consumer products—will start to do better as the economy begins to expand. So when an economy is just starting to recover, consider investing in retail, then materials and industrials.

Tracking Retail Sales Trends

As mentioned, unemployment trends along with consumer confidence naturally affect retail trends. When you start seeing a rise in unemployment, you can deduce that there will be less spending and lower consumer confidence across the board. When that happens, the retail industry becomes questionable. So as an investor you have to look at retail businesses and ask, "Hmm, do I want to be involved in the retail area? Is that a good area to invest in now?" Probably not!

How do you track retail trends, and where do you find data on retail sales? That's easy: the Department of Commerce Census Bureau releases data on retail sales around the middle of each month, usually the 11th to the 15th. The best source for the raw data is the Commerce Department's Census Bureau homepage at www.census.gov/retail/.

Simply stated, this monthly retail sales report provides information on the total receipts at stores that sell durable and nondurable goods. Keep in mind that total consumer spending, of which retail sales comprise half, accounts for two-thirds of the country's GDP, so it's very important to know in what direction retail sales are going. The retail sales number does not include service businesses, so it does not give a 100 percent picture of all consumer spending that takes place over the month. It doesn't tell us anything about health-care services, legal services, yard-care services, education services, or anything like that. It only tracks physical goods like furniture, electronics, and other items that a consumer can purchase. You can keep a pulse on the economy if you closely track consumer confidence and actual behavior—in the form of retail sales. Remember, consumer confidence, or sentiment, refers to how consumers feel about the future of the economy. Consumers often say one thing, but do another, which is why tracking retail sales is helpful. The retail sales number gives you clues as to how the customer is *actually* behaving. Though consumer sentiment is more of a leading indicator, the retail sales number is more of a coincident indicator that tells us what is happening right now with the consumer.

What's nice about the retail sales report is that it breaks down sales across many different types of companies and then shows a total, as well as a separate total called "ex-auto," which excludes automobile sales. Car purchases are an expensive investment for most people, so the government tracks car sales separately from the other smaller items consumers purchase. It's very helpful to see retail sales without adding automobile sales into the total number. The report also breaks out food services into its own category. As always, dig a little deeper than the headline number you might see on TV or read in your newspaper or online.

For example, if you want to know how car sales are doing, the retail sales report gives you the current number of automobiles sold last month, which you can compare to previous months. The report also breaks down retail sales into electronics, sporting goods, clothing stores, department stores, furniture stores, and more. Though it will not show you an individual company's performance, you can get a gauge on how the sales might be faring at leading companies in a particular industry, such as Home Depot (HD) and Lowe's (LOW).

Keep in mind that the retail sales numbers, which are reported in millions of dollars, are estimates based on data from the Advance Monthly Retail Trade Report, Monthly Retail Trade Report, and administrative records. The data spans the current and last five months of reports, including revisions. Retail sales numbers can be adjusted from the previous month, so be sure to see what revisions were made.

Certain financial Web sites present charts of retail sales trends, including information from Bloomberg supplied by Econoday at www.econoday.com or bloomberg.econoday.com. As with any indicator, it's more important to know the trend over the past six months to one year rather than just simply relying on the current number in isolation.

The Winning Investor's Strategy

How do you turn retail sales numbers into action for your portfolio? It can be easy if you practice! Because the retail sales report breaks down sales across different industry groups, you can use it to identify specific areas of the broader economy that may be getting stronger. Just scan the report from the past four months to the current number to see if a particular industry group is continually improving.

Let's take the category of clothing stores/clothing accessory stores as an example. The retail sales report breaks down clothing store sales further, into men's clothing stores, women's clothing stores, and shoe stores. If you see the numbers increasing month to month in this category, you then might look closer at how actual companies that affect the retail sales numbers you are seeing are doing. Remember that the numbers are reported in millions of dollars of sales, so if you see the numbers improving from the past few months to the present—from 8,000 to 9,000 to 10,000, and so on—it means that that industry is reporting estimated sales of $8 million, $9 million, and so forth.

If you notice that sales are improving particularly in men's clothing stores, you might look at a handful of stocks that fit that category, like Joseph A. Banks (JOSB). You would then examine the balance sheet, prior earnings, and other fundamental analysis numbers specific to Joseph A. Banks to see if this might be a company to add to your portfolio (we'll get to all that in the later chapters on analysis). Paying attention to which specific area of retail seems to be growing, or trending higher, is an example of how you might use the retail sales report on a microlevel, or individual stock level.

The total retail sales report (excluding automobiles) also gives us insight into the broad economy. If we are seeing consistent month-to-month increases in retail sales, then that is a sign we are in an economic expansion—a time when you want a large percentage of stocks in your portfolio. On the other hand, if you see a trend of declining retail sales numbers, perhaps when linked to declining consumer sentiment numbers, that would indicate a potential economic decline or a contraction phase. In this case, you may be much more defensive in your portfolio, with a smaller percentage of stocks and a larger percentage of bonds or cash.

If total retail sales continuously increase each month, then that is a signal the consumer is spending money. This could translate into profits for companies, and then to rising stock prices. This is one reason investors pay so much attention to both consumer confidence and retail sales—they are tightly linked. A confident consumer will spend. So pay close attention to the monthly retail sales number, as it can clue you in to what the broader economy is doing, while giving you ideas about stocks to add to your portfolio during economic expansions.

Quick and Dirty Lesson from the Market

Sometimes no matter what the indicators say, you can't always predict or make sense of something that happens. In the first half of 2009, unemployment was high and the economy was not doing so well. But surprisingly the stock price of Joseph A. Banks (JOSB), the men's suits retailer, was doing well. You would think that if workers were being laid off and not going to work, they wouldn't need suits—and they wouldn't have the extra money to buy them anyway, right? Yet Joseph A. Banks' stock went up dramatically in the first half of 2009. You might ask, "How is it possible that a clothing store is doing well?" Well, it's possible that there were more people out of work, so they needed suits for interviews, or it's possible that the cost of fabric and other materials needed to make clothes was much lower than it had been. Either way, Joseph A. Banks' success is a good example of how individual stocks can buck the broader market trend and why it's important to watch stocks individually.

Tracking Real Estate and Housing Indicators

Okay, so now you're tracking unemployment trends, and you're watching retail trends. You also want to monitor real estate trends, because the real estate housing market is another indicator of economic strength (or weakness). There are a number of monthly reports that tell us what's occurring in the real estate market.

The two main indicators are *new housing starts and building permits* and *new home sales*. Like the retail sales report, these are also released by the Census Bureau of the Department of Commerce. Let's look at these one at a time.

New Housing Starts and Building Permits

The more important number to most investors is the new housing starts and building permits, as it is a leading indicator of economic activity. Housing is often the first indicator to turn down or decline before the onset of an economic recession (as happened prior to the 2008 recession). It is also one of the first indicators to turn around and begin to rise prior to a full-blown economic recovery. That makes a lot of sense and we'll see why shortly.

The government releases the housing starts/building permits report toward the middle of each month, usually between the 16th and 20th. You can find it on the Census Bureau's Web site at www .census.gov/starts. The report provides data on both single-family and multifamily dwellings, such as apartments, and breaks it down according to sections of the country—West, Midwest, Northeast, South—so you can see which areas of the country are seeing a growth in new housing starts or which are declining. The government counts a building as "started" when excavation begins. You have to obtain a housing permit before a building can be started, so you can get a view into the future by watching the housing permits number in conjunction with the housing starts. A rise in permits indicates there will probably be a rise in housing starts and vice versa. The Commerce Department actually includes housing permits in its category of leading economic indicators. Though most of the time, once an individual or company goes to the trouble of obtaining a permit for a new building, they will see it through to completion, this is not always the case. That's why we separate permits from starts, and starts from sales.

New Home Sales

The other main real estate indicator to watch is new home sales, which is also reported by the Census Bureau of the Commerce Department. You can find it at the following Web site: www.census.gov/newhomesales. The department reports new home sales at the end of a month or at the very start of a new month, with the new home sales broken down into geographic regions. The report also provides average and median home sale prices, the number of houses on the market, and the supply of unsold homes, which is expressed as the number of months it would take at the current selling rate to work through all the unsold homes.

Here is an example of the summary statement, taken from the March 2010 new home sales report: "The median sales price of new houses sold in March 2010 was $214,000; the average sales price was $258,600. The seasonally adjusted estimate of new houses for sale at the end of March was 228,000. This represents a supply of 6.7 months at the current sales rate." As you can see, the first sentence gives you the information you need. The rest of the report segments the information into regions and gives you the numbers going back over the last year, separated by month so that you can visualize the trend.

Winning Investor's Strategy

As you might suspect, a rise in the number of permits, starts, and new home sales signifies a period of economic expansion, whereas a flat period that then turns into a decline signifies that an economic contraction is developing. Why are these numbers so important to you as an investor? If you own your current home, think back to the big life decisions you made that resulted in you purchasing the house. Would you take out a large mortgage and own your home if you suspected you might get laid off in the future? Or if you felt that you might receive a pay cut or that the economy was headed for troubled times in the future? Probably not! Remember, confident consumers spend. Consumers who are not confident about the future save.

If investors are worried about the state of the economy, they will postpone buying "big-ticket items" like cars and houses. That is another reason we look at automobile sales separately from general retail sales. There's a big difference between buying a shirt and a car, and an even bigger difference in buying a car and a new home.

All things being equal, individuals will make big-ticket purchases when they feel their jobs are secure and that they will be able to keep up with their monthly mortgage payments. This is often the result of a rising or expanding economy.

So how can housing starts be a leading indicator, and how can you put this knowledge to work? Let's assume that we are toward the end of a recession. The economy has been declining over the last few months, unemployment is rising, and things still seem bad. Consumers are saving their money because they fear what's ahead. Eventually, fear will give way to opportunity, and brave souls will venture out and spend money they have been saving. The price of homes most likely has fallen during the recession, and now individuals and investors want to take advantage by purchasing a new or existing home at a reduced price as a potential investment or as a personal dwelling. So we start to notice a stop in the decline month after month in new home sales, permits, and housing starts and a leveling-off in the monthly numbers. Eventually, we may start to see a month-over-month rise in these numbers, which starts slowly and then begins to grow.

What must individuals do when they purchase a new home? That's right! They have to furnish it. So they go out and shop at home-furnishing and general (or specific) retail stores for furniture, rugs, televisions, appliances, and a host of other goods. If this trend expands to the broader economy, we will start to see a leveling-off and then a rise in the retail sales numbers as consumers furnish new homes they just bought. At some point, consumer confidence numbers will start to rise, and we will be turning the corner from a recession to trough (bottom) and then into an early economic recovery phase. The spark that ignited it all may have been housing permits, starts, and new home sale numbers initially turning the corner.

What is the quick and dirty tip for real estate and housing trends? Look at the month-to-month numbers for any signs of growth, leveling-off of growth, decline, or leveling-off of decline, and realize that housing numbers can be leading indicators to the broader economy. If you start to see housing numbers level and then begin to rise, pay close attention to retail sales. You may want to invest in homebuilders such as KB Homes (KBH), Lennar Corporation (LEN), and others as the housing market shows renewed signs of life. Then look to home-goods stores like Lowe's (LOW) and Home Depot (HD), as well as furniture companies, to see if their sales are picking up as a result of the potential turnaround in the real estate market.

In addition to giving you individual names to consider for

your portfolio, the housing and real estate information can also give you a sense of potential turns in the broader economy.

Tracking Materials, Manufacturing, Construction, and Industrial Trends

So far, we've noted that the GDP, the unemployment rate, consumer confidence, retail sales, and housing are key monthly reports that give a big picture view of the health of the economy at present and how it might be faring in the future. There are also a few other indicators to watch that go beyond the consumer and spending trends of the public. For them, we need to look at the production side of the economy, not just the consumer side. *Production* refers to those companies that make the goods and products that consumers buy. The new television we just bought was manufactured by a company that bought electronic and plastic components from other suppliers and then assembled those parts into a finished product. Companies had to produce the plastics and electronics that the TV manufacturer transforms into a TV. Moreover, some companies had to mine the raw materials from the ground, then other companies had to form these raw materials into plastic and electronics that the TV company (Sony, perhaps) bought and fabricated into a TV. The TV had to be sent to a retail store so the consumer could buy it off the shelf. Along the way, there were also transportation companies at all stages of the mining and production that transported the finished goods to market and then to the consumer's home. A lot more goes into a television than you might think!

The new house which a family just purchased underwent a period of building made possible by a construction company. Companies also collect and process raw materials like lumber and steel that go into new homes and the goods that consumers buy. As you might have guessed, there are indicators we can track on the production side of the economy, and these are certainly helpful in assessing the fitness of the economy beyond the consumer.

Industrial Production and Capacity Utilization Report

Let's start with the Industrial Production and Capacity Utilization report. This report, released by the board of governors of the Federal Reserve between the 14th and 17th of each month, tracks two major components of industrial trends in the economy. The report separates activity by specific industry groups, including consumer goods, business equipment, construction, materials, manufacturing, mining, and utilities. You can find the current Industrial Production and Capacity Utilization report at the following Web site (or other sites we have mentioned previously): www.federalreserve .gov/releases/G17/Current/default.htm. It can be helpful to monitor trends in each of these areas in addition to the headline total index numbers.

Industrial Production

The first component, *industrial production*, measures the physical volume of output of the nation's factories, mines, and utilities. The Industrial Production report tells you what's going on behind the scenes to get the goods you buy to your local store. The data are presented both as an index and in percentage changes month to month, making it easier to see the trend in industrial production.

The report is somewhat of a coincident indicator, as it only tells us what is occurring right now in the manufacturing and production side of businesses, not what is about to develop or what has transpired. A rising number indicates that companies are producing more goods to meet the demand of the consumer during an economic expansion; this means more goods purchased, more goods produced, higher corporate profits, higher stock prices, and higher GDP, all of which are signs of a healthy economy in an expansion mode. A decline in industrial production sends the opposite message.

Capacity Utilization Percentage

The second component of the report, the *capacity utilization percentage*, provides an estimate of the extent to which the capital stock of the nation is being used for the production of goods. This percentage rises and falls with the expansion and contraction of the business cycle, with utilization rates higher in expansion phases and lower in contraction phases. Think of 100 percent as full capacity (you'll rarely see 100 percent capacity reported) and 50 percent as half capacity. When the economy bottoms and then begins rising from a recession, production in factories rises, as does the utilization rate of those factories as they move toward full capacity. But as the economy peaks and then starts to fall into a contraction phase, factory production declines, as does the utilization rate.

Think of it this way: the number of factories in the country remains relatively constant. When the economy is contracting in a recession, consumers are purchasing fewer goods than during an expansion, and so factory production slows down to adjust to the decline in demand. Factories in turn lay off workers and reduce production, which decreases the potential capacity of a factory.

Let's say that a particular factory can produce 1,000 widgets or gadgets per day at full capacity. However, now assume that the economy is in recession, and the factory receives fewer than the 1,000 orders per day that it can make with full employment. Perhaps it decreases the rate of production to 600 gadgets per day, making its utilization rate 60 percent of full capacity. When the economy rebounds, the factory will get more orders and then hire new workers and build 800 gadgets per day, which will increase the utilization number to 80 percent. That's a good way to think of what the utilization percentage number means, as you study industrial and economic trends.

Let's take a look at an actual Industrial Production and Capacity Utilization report. The April 15, 2010, report listed the total industrial production index for February 2010 at index number 101.5. The production index number for January 2010 was 101.02. The report listed the percentage change from January to February as 0.03 percent, indicating an expansion in the right direction for economic growth. The index had been rising steadily over the prior months. The report listed the total capacity utilization percentage for February 2010 at 73 percent, which is higher than January's 72.7 percent and higher than December 2009's percentage of 72 percent. The trend was rising, which indicates that as of April 2010, factory production and utilization were increasing month over month, thus signalling that the economy was expanding.

Winning Investor's Strategy

What's nice about the report is that it breaks down production and capacity utilization numbers by industry group, including final products, consumer goods, business equipment, construction, materials, manufacturing, mining, and utilities. Just as with the retail sales report, the breakdown of industry groups makes it easier to determine which sectors or industry groups are showing the greatest strength. This allows you to then look to leading companies in those groups for possible stocks to add to your portfolio during an economic expansion.

If you want to add sector exposure to your portfolio when the manufacturing and industrial numbers are improving, you can use a leading-sector exchange-traded fund (ETF), such as (XLI) for industrials and (XLB) for materials. The quick and dirty tip is to remember that materials represent "things" like raw materials, such as steel, aluminum, copper, and wood, which get manufactured into items you buy, such as chairs, desks, televisions, and cars. You can track these two components of the economy (manufacturing and industrial) separately for more information.

In an economic expansion, consumers and companies will spend more to buy more goods. Companies that produce these goods will have to buy materials to make these goods (from raw material companies) and then manufacture these raw materials into the items that get shipped and transported (another major component of the economy you can track) to stores across the country. If consumers are not spending, then companies will often manufacture less, which means they buy fewer raw materials.

You can also look further into the leading individual stocks that reside in the industrials and materials sectors. For example, the industrials sector includes companies from such industries as building products, construction and engineering, electrical equipment, machinery, and commercial supplies. The materials sector contains stocks that comprise such industries as chemicals, construction materials, containers and packaging, metals and mining, and paper/forest products. Leading companies in the materials sector may include Dow Chemical (DOW) and U.S. Steel Corp (X), Monsanto (MON), Alcoa (AA), and Newmont Mining Corporation (NEM), while leading companies in the industrials sector might include General Electric (GE), United Technologies (UTX), and 3M Company (MMM).

Not only can the Industrial Production and Capacity Utilization Report give you winning ideas of stocks to research, it also gives you a clearer picture of the behind-the-scenes economy. A rising industrial production number and increasing capacity utilization indicate that the broader economy is in an expansion mode, consumers are spending, companies are making more profits, and company share prices may be set to rise. This lets you know that it's time to be invested in stocks. On the other hand, if you continue to see the numbers and percentages stall and then decline month after month, this tells you the economy is contracting, consumers are not spending, companies are not selling as much and thus making less profit, and stock prices will potentially fall. You would want to be more defensive with your portfolio and have a larger percentage of your investments in bonds, cash, or other safe alternates.

Now you can track not just retail sales, but what goes on behind the scenes to get those products to market for consumers to buy. Knowing how to do this can make you a winning investor.

Tracking Trends in Inflation

In chapter 3, we talked about the risk of inflation for investors who stuck their money under the mattress because they were afraid of losing it. Now we'll look at how investors track inflation trends to know when inflation is running at a normal, acceptable pace or whether it is picking up faster than normal, which could lead to some negative effects for the economy. Simply stated, inflation is a rise in the prices we pay for goods and services across the board. A little inflation is normal; a lot of inflation is not. Economists generally accept that an inflation rate of 2 percent to 3 percent is normal in a growing, robust economy. However, anything above 5 percent is considered bad or dangerous for the economy, and the Federal Reserve will take action to combat rapid rises in inflation, usually by raising the federal funds interest rate slightly, which makes the cost of borrowing money more expensive. For now, let's examine two main indicators you can use to track changes in inflation.

The two economic indicators you should use to track inflation are the Producer Price Index (PPI) and the Consumer Price Index (CPI), which are both published by the Bureau of Labor Statistics of the U.S. Department of Labor. The PPI report is released ahead of the CPI report, but both are published toward the first half of the month. The Web sites for these reports are easy to locate:

✦ The Producer Product Index is found at www.bls.gov/ppi/.
✦ The Consumer Product Index is found at www.bls.gov/cpi/.

How do these indexes differ? The producer product index takes into account what companies pay to buy materials, usually raw materials such as wood, crude oil, and so forth, to make the finished goods or products that consumers eventually buy in stores. If inflation is on the rise, it will usually be seen first in the price of the raw materials that companies buy to make products, and they will then increase the price of these products when they go to market to be bought by the consumer.

The consumer product index measures a basket of goods and services that consumers buy at stores. If the price of these goods rises month to month, then that indicates inflation because, while the goods remain the same, it costs more to buy them.

Both indexes show the data as a month-to-month change, given in the form of a percentage. For example, the April 2010 PPI report listed a total producer price index change of 0.7 percent from February, indicating a rise in prices. The April 2010 CPI report listed a total consumer price index change of 0.1 percent from February, which also was a slight rise. As you'll see by looking at the reports, the month-to-month changes can be quite volatile, so it's best to look at the change from a year ago, which also is reported in the data. The 12-month change in the PPI from February 2009 to February 2010 was 4.4 percent, which is slightly higher than the normal 2 percent to 3 percent, but not yet in the alarm zone. The 12-month change in the CPI from February 2009 to

February 2010 was 2.3 percent, which is right in line with an economy that is not running too "hot" on price inflation.

Both reports break down specific segments of the economy to show how different sectors performed. The CPI data divides percentage changes in food, energy, new vehicles, used cars, apparel, medical care, services, and transportation, among others. This can help you pinpoint exactly where the highest changes in prices are occurring. Economists like to exclude food and energy prices from inflation data because these two groups are extremely sensitive to what we call "temporary price shocks," which spike up and then fall back down. For example, if there's a drought in the Midwest, it can send corn and wheat prices higher for a month, but as soon as it rains, those prices often fall right back to where they were. The same can happen if there's an unexpected freeze in Florida, which destroys part of the orange crop. Once the freeze is over, most prices return to normal.

That's also true with energy prices that experience temporary spikes, like after a hurricane hits oil wells in the Gulf of Mexico, or when there are international tensions or an explosion in a major pipeline, such as happened with BP in the Gulf in April 2010. Once the problem "disappears," the price of oil returns back to normal levels. That is partly why you're more likely to see larger spikes and changes in the PPI number each month than in the more stable CPI number, and it explains why you should look at them separately for a more accurate picture.

When we look at inflation, we want to measure the type of inflation that is semi-permanent, not temporary. When wages increase (you can see this in the monthly jobs report, as described earlier), it is a form of inflation that is permanent. Employers generally don't decrease salaries across the board each year, but instead raise them, usually to keep pace with inflation trends.

Winning Investor's Strategy

What's a winning investor to do with this data? The PPI and CPI aren't as effective as the other reports we've mentioned in terms of segmenting out a sector of the economy that's doing very well and then giving you winning ideas of what stocks to consider adding to your portfolio. That doesn't mean the information is not useful though. It's just that inflation data help you see if the economy is growing at a Goldilocks pace: not too fast, not too slow, but just right. The sweet spot is about a constant 2 percent to 3 percent year-over-year change. Anything less than that suggests we're in an economic contraction phase, but anything above suggests that the economy is growing faster than it needs to. In this case, the Federal Reserve may take defensive action to stop inflation; this usually means raising interest rates, which makes borrowing money more expensive.

Use the information from the PPI and CPI report to gauge whether the economy is expanding too fast or just right. You should be invested strongly in stocks in an economic expansion that is not showing great signs of inflation (as opposed to a quickly rising economy that is also experiencing a high inflation rate). Be cautious and perhaps more defensive if you see major signs that inflation is getting out of control—above the 5 percent level or more per year. The Federal Reserve usually does a good job of not letting that happen, but realize that it must take evasive action if inflation does rise more than normal. The Federal Reserve raises interest rates to slow some of the excessive economic growth, and that means higher interest rates across the board.

Tracking Trends in Energy

Energy production and energy consumption are coincident indicators: they provide information about the current state of the economy, or where in the economic cycle we are. Information on energy production and consumption comes out every week in reports on the current levels of oil inventories; see www.energy.gov, the Department of Energy Web site, for the best source of this information. When looking at that information, consider if the oil inventory appears to be building or falling; that's the indicator. If you see a buildup in inventories every single week, then that could be a signal that there's not as much consumption going on. This information is an identifier of what's transpiring in our economy, because fuel is used to transport people, goods, and so on. So if consumption of oil is declining, that might mean fewer goods are being transported, which might indicate a slowdown in the economy.

Also keep in mind that energy is used in a couple of ways. First of all, it's used for heating, and second, it's used for transportation and manufacturing. If energy use is increasing, you need to consider whether people are traveling more. Traditionally, the use of energy correlates highly with the movement of an economy, so if energy usage has decreased, then the economy is probably not doing well either. People aren't going anywhere, and goods aren't traveling as much. Furthermore, if goods aren't traveling anywhere, that means they're not being bought, they're not being manufactured, or they're not being mined. That's not a good sign.

The Winning Investor's Strategy

What can you do with this information, and how should it influence your winning investment strategy? Well, if you notice that energy usage is increasing over time, you can infer that the economy may be growing or expanding. You can also consider adding energy investments to your portfolio. The simplest way to do so when you see an upward trend in energy use is to purchase a major exchange-traded fund like (XLE), the AMEX sector ETF that many investors use as a proxy for companies that are heavily exposed to the energy market, like Exxon Mobil (XOM), Chevron Corporation (CVX), Schlumberger (SLB), Devon Energy Corporation (DVN), Halliburton (HAL), and Valero (VLO). Remember that investing in an exchange-traded fund is like buying shares in many companies; it spreads risk through diversification, whereas if you purchase a single stock, you are investing only in that one company. You can also do your own research to find a handful of companies that are either outperforming other energy-related companies, or have better balance sheets or fundamental statistics than other companies. Like all sectors, there are leading and lagging companies, and if you do your research, you can invest in the winners.

Quick and Dirty Tip

Keep in mind that fuel is seasonal. In the summer, because you travel more, you use more fuel than you do in winter, unless you happen to live in a very cold climate. In that case, you might increase energy usage in both summer (for car and airline travel) and winter (for heating your home). Consider this when assessing the reports. A change in the price of energy at certain points in the year is called "seasonality" and is normal. Be sure to factor seasonal trends into your analysis, and note whether prices are differing sharply from seasonal norms.

You also have to watch for extremes. If you've invested in crude oil and prices rise too quickly, it is possible that the bubble could deflate quickly. Commodities, like oil, can have what we call "bubbles": prices suddenly rise straight up, but then the bubble bursts and prices fall just as quickly as they rose. Winning Investors prefer stability, not volatility, in our investments. A stable rise in energy prices is generally safe, whereas a meteoric rise is not.

Think about why this is so. Companies and individuals have to budget how much they spend each month in fuel. Let's say that gas costs $3 per gallon, while oil is near $80 per barrel. Let's also assume that during each of the past six months, the price of crude oil and the price we pay at the gas station have been increasing steadily like Goldilocks—not too fast, not too slow. However, all of a sudden you see crude oil prices jump to $90, then $100, per barrel in a single month and gas at the pump rises to $3.50. The next month you see a similar, larger than normal rise. Nobody took into account a sharp rise in the price of crude oil, which translates into higher fuel and energy costs across the whole economy.

Shares of Exxon-Mobil (XOM) and other oil/energy companies may also rise sharply and suddenly. For those who hold these stocks, that's a good thing, but is it a good thing for the economy? In a quick answer, no.

Why? Because everyone will have to pay more for an expense they didn't budget for; even if they did budget for it, they are going to have to spend more money anyway. If the price gets too high, individuals and companies will have to cut back on spending in other areas, which can lead to the peak of the economy and the onset of a contraction-phase spiral. A company may have to lay off workers or cut back on business to account for the sharp rise in energy prices, just like individuals will have to sacrifice to fuel their vehicles. When companies and individuals cut back on their spending, the economy contracts. Companies lay off workers, and so those people cannot spend money on goods like televisions, dining-room furniture, vacations, and new homes. This eventually leads to a decline in other parts of the economy, which leads to more layoffs and a general decline in sales. Now a decline in the economy begins that could spiral for some time to come. This actually happened in the summer of 2008 when gas/oil prices rose dramatically. People were spending so much on gas that they had less money to spend elsewhere. It's not that high energy prices cause recessions, but there is a high correlation between large spikes in energy prices and slowdowns in economic activity. Eventually, as consumers and companies cut back, both spend less on energy as they drive to fewer locations and facilities are closed. As a result, energy prices fall along with the economy.

So, in a word, you have to be very careful. There is a delicate balance between the price of oil and how the economy is going. If you see signs that something is out of whack, such as a sudden rise in the price of oil that stays high for many months, then think carefully about what other economic numbers are doing. Start taking profits, and reduce your exposure to energy. If you're invested, for example, in Exxon (XOM) or other oil stock, in an oil ETF, or in coal companies, consider selling all or at least part of those holdings. And don't consider buying any more of those investments until pricing becomes more attractive. Remember, no one ever gets hurt taking a profit.

Where to Find Information to Track Economic Trends

Earlier in this chapter, I mentioned a few good Web sites providing information that's updated regularly so you can track economic trends. Following are a few other sites that can help you track important economic trends, and make investment decisions.

For real estate, check out these sites:

✦ www.realtor.org: the National Association of Realtors.
✦ www.bloomberg.com
✦ www.briefing.com
✦ finance.yahoo.com: Yahoo!'s money site.
✦ moneycentral.msn.com: MSN's money site.

For the economy in general, see:

✦ www.economy.com
✦ www.Dismal.com
✦ www.stlouisfed.org: see the "Research" page.
✦ www.briefing.com

The Bottom Line

The point of this chapter on key indicators you should watch and how to get winning ideas on what you might want to invest in is that *this is the beginning of the investment process*. The information just presented helps you evaluate the state of the economy so that you can make better, more informed investment decisions—decisions about whether to be (1) more offensive (by trying to make money when signals are "all clear" and pointing to economic expansion) or (2) more defensive (by trying to protect the money you have when signals are not clear or are pointing to economic contraction). It also helps you get ideas for the kinds of particular winning investments you might want to make. That's a double benefit!

Admittedly, it's not always easy to interpret indicators and know exactly where we are in the economic cycle. Even economists differ on how the economy is doing and where it is moving at any given time. Nevertheless, you have to decipher the information so that you can make some investing decisions. If you decide that you just don't know so you're not going to do anything, that won't get you anywhere. If you simply shove your money under your mattress, that's not going to help it grow.

Be sure to look at all the different economic indicators described in this chapter so you can get an overview on the health of the economy. In general, when you look at any of these economic indicators, including employment, retail, the producer price index, consumer confidence, and so on, and believe the economy is improving and that consumers and companies are doing much better, then you should probably *add* to your investments. In contrast, if the trends you're tracking and indicators you're watching signal that the economy is trending down, you probably won't want to buy anything new. You may even want to sell stock in your portfolio and purchase bonds or bond ETFs.

The bottom line is that when you've been monitoring indicators and tracking trends, you'll have a big picture of the economy and a sense of how it's doing. That's when you'll need to develop your game plan and strategy. For that, let's turn to chapter 5.

Quick and Dirty Tip

There may be times when the U.S. economy is doing poorly, but the overseas economies, like Asia's, are doing very well. You have to look at the global picture to see where the best winning investment opportunities are. Compare overseas indexes or ETFs to what the Dow Jones or S&P 500 indexes in the United States are doing.

5

How to Invest in the Market

How to Invest When the Market Is Down, Up, Volatile, and Neutral

Now that you know about the economic cycle, what economic indicators to track, and how they can give you ideas for what to invest in, let's look at how to invest during different types of markets. We already know about the economic cycle and the four main economic stages. Well, the stock market has three basic stages, or conditions, of its own.*

1. **a rally**: a market that's trending up
2. **a correction**: a market that's trending down
3. **a sideways market**: a market with no clear trend

---

*This discussion of markets also applies to individual stocks, which can have similar movements.

It is a good idea to have a game plan for each of these markets, as well as a plan for when the market is extremely volatile—that is, when stock prices are changing, or moving, faster than normal. In a normal environment, you may see price movements of 2 percent per week depending on the stock, whereas in a volatile environment, you may see a 2 percent move or greater in a single day. It's easiest to define *volatility* as rapidly moving prices. *Volatile markets* are identified by multiple days of high percentage moves in individual stocks or in the indexes themselves. Your goal is to be ready for anything the market can, and quite possibly will throw at you.

First, of course, you need to recognize what the trend is, which can be tricky. Market direction is not always linear. There really is no situation when you can say, "Because the market went that way for thirty days, it has to reverse." In a sideways market, it is often difficult to determine whether it may eventually break up or down. You need to be able to look at the market objectively and figure out what it's doing now and where it is most likely going to go. This information will help you to decide how to position your investments.

Why You Need to Pay Attention to the Market

People write, call, and ask me all the time, "What's the market going to do next? What should I invest in now?" During market corrections, when the market is trending down, most everyone wants to protect their money. Yet during market rallies, when the market is trending up, many investors don't give much thought to protecting their money; they just want to make money. When the market is up and times are good, investors become complacent, even though they promised they were going to take more control of their investments. Being complacent—in good markets as well as bad—is not a great way to manage your money, because you never know exactly when the trend is going to change. That's why it's good to keep on top of the latest signals and recent information that might alert you that there is a change occurring, either in sentiment or in market conditions.

In this chapter I'll first tell you what these signals are and how you can use them to figure out what the market is doing. Then I'll give you tips on how to invest in different types of markets: up, down, neutral, and extremely volatile. That way, you'll have a plan in place when you identify which way the market (or a stock) is moving.

How to Identify the Market Trend

In all of our examples, we will use the S&P 500 index as our benchmark index to refer to the market (see chapter 2 if you need a refresher on the S&P 500). The charts I'll use as examples will show the weekly movements of the S&P 500 index. Many of these charts will also include the fifty-week moving average as a reference. A *moving average* is simply the average price of a stock price over a given period, which is plotted on a stock chart as a line. Each day, the average spits out the oldest value and plugs in the most recent data and chugs along as a line. There are many different moving averages investors like to watch, including the twenty- , fifty- , and two hundred-day moving averages. The fifty-week moving average is another one to watch because it's the average closing value of a security over almost a year—the last fifty weeks. Thus, the average represents the average price of the market over the last year. When looking at a stock chart with the fifty-week moving average, you will want to know if the price is above its annual average price or below it. I'll describe how moving averages work and how to read charts in more detail in chapter 10 on technical analysis.

As mentioned previously, there are three main trends, or market conditions.

✦ Markets are in an **uptrend** (rally) if you can observe higher price highs and higher price lows. If the price is above the fifty-week moving average on the weekly chart or ten-month moving average on the monthly chart, and the slope of the respective moving average is rising. (Bull Market)

✦ Markets are in a **downtrend** (correction) if you can observe lower price lows and lower price highs. If the price is beneath the fifty-week moving average on the weekly chart or ten-month moving average on the monthly chart, and the slope of the respective moving average is falling. (Bear Market)

✦ Markets are in a **neutral or flat trend** (sideways) when you see roughly equal price highs and price lows that form a rectangle or sideways horizontal line, and the respective moving averages are flat along with price.

Market Uptrend

Let's now see examples of the S&P 500 index in an uptrend so we can visualize what an uptrend looks like. Figure 2 shows us the S&P 500 index from mid-2003 until mid-2008. The thin line is the fifty-week moving average. You can see that price broke above the fifty-week moving average in mid-2003 (at the left) and continued to move higher—with the exception of a few dips under the moving average, which is nothing to worry about. Uptrends are bull markets and show strength, when it is often the safest time to be invested in the stock market.

Downtrend

Let's shift gears to see the opposite pattern, that of a downtrend on the price chart of the S&P 500. Figure 3 shows us the entire downtrend, or bear market, from 2000 to 2003. In contrast to the uptrend, here we see the S&P 500 index crossing solidly under

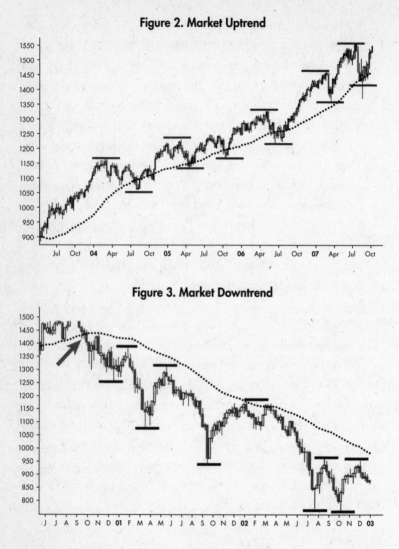

Figure 2. Market Uptrend

Figure 3. Market Downtrend

the fifty-week moving average in October 2000 and then remaining under that average for the duration of the chart, with the exception of a small blip in early 2002. Note the slope of the fifty-week moving average itself is moving down as the average price of the index declines month to month.

During a downtrend, it is not safe to be fully invested in stocks, and you generally should be defensive and hold most of your portfolio in cash or bonds. The share price of 3 out of 4 of the most fundamentally solid companies often declines during a bear market, so it's best not to attempt to pick out the few market gems that will go against the broad market trend. When the market is in a bearish downtrend, it's best to protect your capital and be defensive.

Note also how the trend began to change in late 2002 as the price began to form equal swing highs and swing lows. This was the beginning of a flat, or range-bound market, which is the next example of a price trend.

Flat, or Range-bound, Market

An uptrend moves forward with higher price highs and higher price lows, and a downtrend moves forward with lower price lows and lower price highs. But a neutral or range-bound market moves with roughly equal price highs and lows that usually form a rectangle chart pattern. The moving average starts to flatten as price continues to be range-bound.

Figure 4 shows us a market in transition, also known as a neutral, flat, or consolidating trend. The bear market of 2000–2003 ended in a year-long neutral, or range-bound, trend that began in mid-2002 and lasted until mid-2003. As you can see, the price moved both up and down without a discernable long-term trend.

It takes a lot of investment skill and work to profit during a market in transition, because it is difficult to know if the market is pausing and will continue its uptrend, or if it is transitioning into a downward or bear market. When the market breaks out of its boundaries, as it did in early 2008, it is often a sign that the market is beginning a new trend; in this case, the new trend began to move lower, which then led to the bear market of 2008,

Figure 4. Flat Market

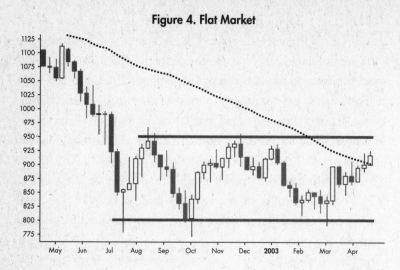

where it was best to be defensive and raise cash in your portfolio by selling stocks.

Remember, when assessing a trend, do not look at the tiny details, but focus instead on the larger picture that the chart is revealing. Trends can last two to four years or more, so don't think that a trend will magically end once you see one has developed. Changing a trend on the large scale is like a big train changing directions. The train first has to slow down before it can turn around, and this slowdown and turnaround are most often reflected on the charts through a market in transition, or a range-bound market.

By watching the weekly or monthly chart of the S&P 500, Dow Jones, or NASDAQ indexes, along with the fifty-week or ten-month moving average, you can get a good sense as to whether the market is currently in an uptrend, downtrend, or sideways range-bound market. Then you can adjust your investment strategies accordingly, which is what we'll get to next.

How Should You Invest When the Market Is Going Down?

Before discussing strategies for investing in a down-trending market, I should mention that those investors who follow the buy-and-hold theory (discussed in chapter 1) don't believe they need to do anything differently during a downtrend. They believe it doesn't matter what the market is doing because they're in it for the long haul—and their theory banks on the hope that their investments will be a lot higher in the future than they are now. But here again is why I don't advocate this theory: the lesson we learned in the aftermath of the financial meltdown of 2007–2008 was that buy-and-hold does not work when you don't have a long-term time horizon. If you don't need the money from your investments now and can wait for the market to recover, you might be okay. But what happens if you're invested in the market now, and you want to retire? Those people who were retired, or who wanted to retire, in 2007–2008, and who lost 30 percent to 40 percent of their total net worth, were probably not pleased with their buy-and-hold strategy. How we can more actively protect our investments? During down markets, or market corrections, investors are often scared that they may lose money. Basically, these are times when it's very difficult to invest—whether you're an individual managing your own money, a professional investment advisor, or a financial planner who's managing other people's money. It's a tough time because there are many unknowns, more so than when the market is just bounding along, a little bit up, a little bit down, and so forth.

Here is a little secret: even many professional money managers don't really know what to do in a market that keeps moving lower and lower. Investing experts understand that at times markets need to pause. They simply need to cool every once in a while, to come down a little bit. They need to kind of rest before they can go up again. A down market is called a correction because it's often the market's way of resetting itself when stock prices have been much higher than the stocks are really worth. That's not an absolute, but generally speaking, that's what we've seen historically. Nevertheless, the unknowns of a market and the massive down-market moves sometimes make it difficult to implement sound investment decisions. In these instances, you have to think as unemotionally as you can—not recklessly or spontaneously, but unemotionally, and act on a pre-determined plan. It's important to have a plan ahead of time. That way, you don't have to make decisions in the heat of the moment in order to protect yourself from large losses. Suppose your portfolio is fully invested in stocks, and you don't sell before a stock-market crash. In that case, you'll watch your portfolio wither away, while trying to do your best to hold on to whatever is still there. We don't want that to happen.

The first issue to think about during a market that is correcting or consolidating is not how to make new investments but how to protect your existing investments. Focus on protecting your investments because you don't know when the end of that correction will be until sometime after the market starts to rebound. If you have a plan before the event occurs, you will be ready to act appropriately. It is not what you make, but rather what you keep, that is the creed of successful investors.

Use Sell Stops to Protect Your Portfolio

As mentioned, during a down market you shouldn't be thinking about new stocks to buy; you should be focusing instead on protecting your existing investments. One way to do this is by using *sell stops*, which are automatic orders to sell a stock once the price of the stock reaches a specified price. They are also called *hard stops*. When it first becomes apparent that stocks are falling, that the market and the economy are slowing down, and that your personal portfolio is starting to decrease in value, you should consider sell stops. Be sure to do so before the market really starts to drop, or it will be too late. Before the stock begins falling and bottoms out, you should decide at what price you would sell. Let's say you're invested in a stock—for example, Microsoft (MSFT), Pfizer (PFE), Coca-Cola (KO), or GE (GE)—that's trading at $50 a share, and you see that the market is trending downward. You might say, "Okay, if this stock goes down to $45 a share, which is a 10 percent reduction in its value, I don't want to be invested in it anymore. Instead, I want to sell." If that's what you decide, you can put in an automatic sell stop that says if the stock falls to $45, you're out. This is a simple example, but that's the basic idea. Sell stops protect you from losing money beyond a certain point. Most brokerage houses can help you implement this strategy.

Sell stops help to limit your losses because they take the emotion out of investing. You decide in advance when you're going to sell, and then it's done automatically. You won't be able to dither or decide not to sell because the stock is your favorite. Almost everyone has a favorite stock that they invest in, and even though its price might be decreasing, they just won't let go of it. Don't let this happen to you. Love a stock as long as it loves you; when that changes, it may be to time to find another sweetheart.

Quick and Dirty Tip

You should *not* try to get back the money you've lost in a down market. That is the same mistake that gamblers make: they stay in the game, hoping to recoup their money, instead of simply accepting that they've lost some money and walking away from the table before they lose any more. Don't chase the market; instead, use sell stops to help you walk away before you lose more money! Remember, hope is not an investment strategy.

Soft Stops

Sometimes we use what we call *soft stops*, because hard stops can occasionally be problematic. Just recently, I was looking at a stock that had been priced above $13 a share, when it suddenly dropped to $12.02 right before my eyes. That surprised me, and I wondered what happened. Sure enough, soon after it dropped to almost $12, the price started coming back up to $13—and then it went even higher. Now suppose you owned shares of that stock, and you had a hard stop in place to sell if that stock dropped below $13 a share. That hard stop would have triggered an automatic sell order, and you would have sold your shares even though the price rebounded to above your sell-stop limit in the same day. (In fact, the reason the stock dropped so fast may have been that a series of sell stops hit and drove the price down.)

With a soft stop, you still decide that you want to sell if the stock price drops to $13, but before you automatically sell, you have an opportunity to look at the specifics of what's happening to the price before going through with the sale. Essentially, a soft stop requires you to acknowledge that you really want to sell. The only problem with soft stops is that unlike hard stops, they don't prevent emotion from getting in the way. In other words, the only negative with soft stops is that you can override them.

Essentially, a soft stop is used to confirm that all the market conditions you were concerned about have been met, and if so, that you will still sell that particular investment.

In addition, there are other things you can do, including using stop limits, buy limits, and buy stops, but these are beyond the scope of this book. (For details, you might want to refer to www.investopedia.com, or Jordan Goodman's *Everyone's Money Book*, which offers almost a thousand pages of almost everything you would ever want to know about money.)

Protecting Your Portfolio by Hedging

During a down market you should also be hedging, which I touched on in chapter 3. *Hedging* essentially means finding investments that will work inversely to what the markets are doing, and it's one way you can protect your portfolio beyond the simple diversification of owning a mix of stocks. There are plenty of ETFs and other investment vehicles that can help you hedge. Let's take a look at a specific example of how this can work.

Meet Carlos. Carlos has a fully invested portfolio—that is, all of the money he has to invest is invested in something. He's owns five stocks: JP Morgan (JPM), IBM (IBM), Walmart (WMT), International Paper (IP), and Exxon Mobil (XOM). His portfolio is worth $100,000. Carlos doesn't want to sell his stocks, even though his research leads him to conclude that the stock market is going to decline 20 percent in the next month. He can't diversify by just adding different stocks in different sectors. Even if he diversifies, diversifies, and diversifies some more, if the stock market is moving down in value, his investments will most likely follow in the same direction, no matter how "good" the stocks are. Instead, what Carlos should do is hedge the entire stock market. How can he do this? One way is to buy an inverse ETF, which you'll remember is an ETF that gains value as the market goes down. In this case, Carlos wants to buy an inverse ETF of the S&P 500. If the S&P 500 drops, the stocks Carlos owns will most likely drop too, but his investment in the inverse ETF will profit. He hedges so that the effect of the entire stock market moving down won't hurt his portfolio—at least not as badly. The goal of hedging is to reduce the systematic risk in one's portfolio, and because Carlos owns stocks, his whole portfolio is in the stock market and so that's what he hedges. If he has a "perfect" hedge when the stock market goes down, his hedge goes up, one for one. (Note that this is a perfect hedge; most will not hedge 1:1.)

In addition to these 1:1 inverse ETFs, there are *inverse-leveraged ETFs*. These funds, which return double or triple the percentage gains or losses of a standard ETF, can increase your returns because they're leveraged 2:1 or 3:1. It's like getting more bang for your buck. That might sound confusing, but it's actually very simple. Suppose you invest in UltraShort S&P500 ProShares (symbol SDS), which is a two-times inverse-leveraged S&P 500 (that is, it's 2:1). In other words, when the S&P 500 index goes *up* 10 percent, SDS should go *down* 20 percent. Therefore, if you have $1,000 invested in the S&P 500 index when it goes up 10 percent, you'll have $1,100. However, the other $1,000 that you invested in SDS will now be worth only $800 because it went down 20 percent, and your original $2,000 is now worth only $1,900 ($1,100 from your investment in the S&P 500 and $800 from your investment in SDS).

On the plus side, with a two-times inverse-leveraged ETF, if the S&P 500 index goes *down* 10 percent, SDS goes *up* 20 percent, so your $1,000 in the S&P 500 index is now worth only $900, but your $1,000 invested in SDS is now worth $1,200, for a total of $2,100.

This might seem complicated, but it's not. All you're looking to accomplish is to lose as little as possible during times of market corrections. The whole point of hedging is to make sure that if losses are inevitable, then you can at least soften their effect or temporarily offset them with the short hedge positions. Think of a hedge as something in your portfolio that will potentially move up against the downward trend of the general markets. In general, hedging is not something that the average investor will do, because it's a fairly sophisticated approach to investing, and it's not for novices. Learn as much as you can about hedging before trying it, and consider starting off small for your first few hedges to see how it works out for you.

Why Buying Stocks in a Down Market Is Not a Good Idea

When the market is moving down, you'll likely hear some people saying that now is a great time to buy. "Stocks are at a deep discount; the entire market is on sale," they might say. My response to that advice is that it's great that all stocks are priced low, and you can definitely consider buying, but first you need to research each individual investment and decide whether it is worth even that reduced price.

Never cave in to advice you get from other investors and pundits. Here's why: back in late December 2008, a client asked me, "Andrew, why are you selling my stocks? All my friends say it's time to buy." I found out that my client and his golfing buddies had been talking about how stocks were cheaper and therefore on sale. Without any further research, his friends simply decided, "Hey, it's a good time to buy because the market is down and stock prices are lower." They may have been right, but we all know what happened next—the stock market plummeted. You don't know when a correction is over until it's really over, and you can look back and see where exactly the turnaround began. That's why buying during a downturn can be risky. You may think the market has reached the bottom, but it may still continue dropping. So to recap: my advice in a market downturn is that most people shouldn't make any new stock purchases and should instead focus on protecting their existing investments. Now let's take a look at the opposite situation: what to do when the market is up or moving up.

How Should You Invest in an Up Market?

When the market is trending up, it's generally a good time to consider making new investments. In an up market, two things typically happen. First, a rising tide tends to raise all ships. And second, a rising market can even lift the price of a stock that hasn't been performing well—even if it has weak fundamentals and/or lousy technicals (which I'll explain in chapters 8 and 9)—because investors are voraciously investing. Therefore, in a rising market you don't have to be as discriminating about what you're investing in, though you should still be disciplined and give yourself the best opportunity to make money on your investments. Don't just pick an investment at random.

A good move for average investors in a rising stock market is to invest in ETFs and other broad-based investment vehicles, so they don't have to judge each individual stock. After all, mutual funds are broad-based investment vehicles managed by investment professionals who select a basket of stocks that are expected to outperform the market index itself. An ETF is another broad-based investment vehicle that seeks to match as close as possible to what the underlying index, like the S&P 500, returns. If the market is generally in an uptrend, then you can easily benefit by investing in a particular market or sector, whether it's a fund from Vanguard (one of the world's largest investment management companies); or a sector-specific ETF that invests in companies in the technology sector, retail sector, or energy sector; or even an index fund like the DIA, QQQQ, or SPY. You could even invest in an extended-market ETF like the Vanguard Total Stock Market ETF (VTI) which tracks the performance of a benchmark index that measures the returns of the overall stock market.

When you invest this way, instead of investing in individual stocks or other vehicles, you don't have to worry about things like product recalls, or other events that have a negative effect on a specific company and therefore on its stock price. Also, you don't need to keep current on which market sectors are moving up, because these cover a broad range of sectors. You don't have to be trapped into investing in only one specific area.

In other words, during a bull market you don't need to do as much quantitative, fundamental, or technical analysis (I'll get to these in chapters 7 to 9). Instead, you can be a little less discriminating and a little more relaxed about the process. This is especially helpful for individual investors—including beginners. If you're a beginner, the best time to start being an active investor is when the markets are trending up. Research and discover the stocks you believe have the greatest potential, and the sectors you like the most. Then invest in those, along with broad-based ETFs/funds.

There's really not much more to know about how to invest in an uptrending market. It's a lot easier to be invested in a market during an economic recovery and uptrending market. When the stock market is continually and steadily trending higher, then all sectors and stocks *should* generally benefit. There are always exceptions, of course, but those are usually in individual companies with poorer fundamentals or other company-specific troubles that are not allowing the companies to participate in a broader bull market.

Also keep in mind that you still need to watch the market closely enough to be able to determine when it turns or changes direction. That's when you'll have to start thinking about putting on a short-term hedge—if you believe the uptrend will continue in the future, but that we might hit a rough patch in the next month or two. Don't sell everything, but be somewhat defensive.

Remember that nothing goes straight up. Think of ice skating, for example: most people can probably ice-skate very well *in a straight line*. However, as soon as they need to turn or change direction, things get a little dangerous, and they start to fall down. The same is true of investing: everybody is a genius when they're invested in a rising market. But you need to know when the tide turns, which you can do by watching key moving averages on a price chart as well as following the broader economic picture. If the consumer is confident and spending, companies are hiring workers (so unemployment is not a concern), and factories are increasing production and capacity utilization—along with a host of other rising economic indicators—then you can be confident that the stock market will continue to rise. However, if you start to see pauses or leveling-off in some of these indicators, or you begin to see declines in them, such as a lower level of consumer confidence, lower retail sales, and reduced industrial production or capacity utilization, along with rising unemployment, then the market may be peaking and we could be facing a decline. Always watch the two hundred-day moving average on a stock or a market. The two hundred-day moving average is like the fifty-week moving average. Instead of tracking the past fifty weeks, it tracks the past two hundred days. It's usually a bad sign when a price falls under this average.

The economy is like a big train moving forward. A train first needs to slow down before it stops and then turns around in the other direction. If you start to see a slowdown in the economy, then you can suspect that we might be in for a contraction phase, especially if we've been in an expansion phase for more than a few years without a meaningful sell-off or down market in stocks.

Now let's talk about how to invest during a sideways market.

How to Invest in a Sideways Market: When There's No Trend

The so-called sideways market is a much more difficult trend to assess, because it can go in either direction (hence the name), and just about anything can happen. As mentioned earlier, a sideways market will go up and down, but it doesn't move substantially in either direction. That said, a sideways market may, for example, go down 5 percent, then up 5 percent; or it may go down 5 percent, then up 2 percent, then down 1 percent, and then up 4 percent. A sideways market is often not as lengthy as a bull market. It typically occurs between a bull and a bear market, but it's much more contracted than either of those because usually the market goes in one direction or another. So how should you invest in a sideways market? You might consider adding new positions to your portfolio, but you should also focus on protecting your current investments as well.

When you're thinking about buying, look for quality investments—the best of the best—because when there's no trend and no discernible movement in either direction, you should be very selective in your choices. Invest in stocks or sectors that have been the most solid in either the upturn or the downturn. In a sideways market, you should buy cautiously. Because it's not moving clearly in one direction, it's more difficult to invest in a sideways market; you can't make money (or even avoid losing money) just by being invested in broad-based investments. If you have only broad-based investments such as index ETFs like the SPY, which is like simultaneously investing in five hundred stocks, you're essentially going nowhere during a sideways market. That's because five hundred stocks make up that index, and during a sideways market, some stocks are rising, others are falling, and others are truly going sideways as well. During a bull market, almost all stocks are rising, with few stocks going down and few stocks going sideways. In a bear market, the majority of stocks in a broad-based ETF are often going down, with very few stocks in the index moving up or sideways.

As mentioned, you can classify stocks by the sectors they are in. Amazon (AMZN) and Google (GOOG) would be in the technology sector, whereas Exxon Mobil (XOM) and Chevron (CVX) would be in the energy sector. Specific sectors might be doing well, while others are not doing as well during a sideways market. In a bull market, however, almost all sectors will be rising together, just as in a bear market almost all sectors will be falling together. You might consider investing in sector-specific ETFs instead of a broad-based market ETF (such as the SPY) during a sideways market, buying those sector ETFs (like XLK for technology, XLV for health care, and XLI for industrials) that are rising and avoiding sectors that are falling. In a sideways market, you need to be diligent when buying individual securities because each stock may be going up or down for a different reason.

Remember, a stock price can move dramatically, based on a number of factors: a company could have an amazing innovation, a new product, a change of leadership, or a new partnership. Or the company may be a takeover candidate. When any of these things happens, it can have a dramatic effect on the price of the company's stock. However, does that mean there will be a similar boost for the whole sector? No. During a sideways market, you have to do your research to find those stocks with superior fundamentals and a rising trend on their individual stock charts and invest in those. It's very easy to buy stocks that are rising when the whole market and all sectors are rising, but it's more difficult to do in a sideways market. It just means you have to do a lot of homework!

That's not to say one sector of the stock market can't trend together. There may, in fact, be things that benefit or harm an entire sector even in a sideways market. For example, if new legislation allows for tax credits to for-profit schools, then that entire sector may suddenly benefit. Or the opposite may happen. Suppose there's an outbreak of E. coli in poultry. That can affect the whole sector involved in the poultry business, and other stocks in that sector may get hit pretty hard. Then, depending on how big or widespread the problem is, it might affect the corn market, because poultry eat corn, and if poultry sales are down, there may not be as much demand for corn feed.

There are a host of examples of outside forces that can affect certain sectors positively and negatively, that only affect stocks in certain sectors. You have to watch not only the fundamentals for the companies you're invested in, but also major news events that are unique to the sector to which your stocks belong. News events may affect a certain sector, but leave the broader market untouched, which presents unique opportunities and challenges for you. It's more important to watch big news events, like outbreaks of swine flu, E. coli, hurricanes, oil spills, financial reform, and housing market news, during a sideways market environment than during an up-trending or down-trending market.

All of these examples illustrate that in a sideways market, it's important to be more discriminating and to invest more actively, so you can continue to make money on your investments. In general, sideways markets benefit good stock pickers and good market timers. Market timing is very difficult to do but *in theory*—and I can't emphasize that enough—in theory, you can make money if you can do extra homework, stay on top of the news, watch basic developments on stock charts, and avoid getting greedy. This means you take profits when you have them instead of trying to hold on for very big gains and then letting a winner drop back down into a loss. In a sideways market, your opportunities are limited, and you really have to be on your toes. You can't just "hold and hope" as you can in a steadily rising bull market with the economy clearly in an expansion mode. During a sideways market, you may have to use hedging measures at times, but don't rush out and sell your entire portfolio.

Remember, a sideways market is not a bear market, in which

case you should sell most of your stock portfolio and concentrate in bonds or cash. That's the way to turn a sideways market into a volatility fest, which would be a great way to invest for someone who is looking to move in and out of the markets, based on market timing and technical analysis (which will be covered more in chapter 9).

How to Invest in an Extremely Volatile Market

An *extremely volatile market* is one that has wide price fluctuations and moves wildly up and down. Many investors get freaked out and often panic when the market is volatile because they find it very difficult to determine what direction the market is moving in. "Should I buy?" they ask. "Should I sell? Should I hold? What should I do?" There is no clear-cut answer in this type of market environment. Since 2008, the markets have been performing like nothing many of us have ever seen in our lifetimes, which is why so many people keep looking back to the crash of 1929 and the Depression of the 1930s, and comparing them to 2008. If you asked me how to invest in a volatile market, however, I would say you have one of three choices. You stay in and hope for the best, you get out of the stock market altogether, or you trade actively.

If you decide to stay in and hope for the best, then you're betting that the market will rebound in the long term, and you need to have enough years and patience so you can ride out the bad times. Also, you need to deal with the fact that you may lose a good amount of money along the way, which may cause you great pain, but again you chose to simply hope for the best. The S&P 500 fell almost 60 percent from its October 2007 peak to its March 2009 low; that was a major loss for investors who rode the entire bear market to the eventual low. We know—although not with absolute assurance—that ten or fifteen years from now, stocks in general *should* be higher than they are today. If you can stay in long enough to ride out the volatile market, you may be okay. However, investors who need money from their investments *during* the next five to ten years can't afford to "stay in and hope for the best" because they don't have a enough time to wait. If you are the type who cannot tolerate the potential for such large losses, then you can always concentrate your portfolio in bonds, CDs, or other safe assets that will not lose as much, but will also not gain as much. And although that can be frustrating, remember that you shouldn't be heavily weighted in the stock market if you don't have enough time to ride out the bumps along the way.

Your other choice is to back away from a volatile market and not to invest at all. Take your money out of the stock market—sell everything—and be done with it. Sit on the sidelines until you get a signal that you are more confident about. For example, when you finally see the market leveling off and fundamentals and economic indicators improving, then you might think about getting back in . . . slowly.

Volatility Isn't Necessarily Bad: There's Good Volatility and Bad Volatility

There's one more interesting point about volatility. Most people think volatility is "bad," because they look only at markets that are moving—for example, up 4 and then down 5, and so forth. There can also be upside volatility, where the market can be moving up 1, up 5, up 2, up 7, up 2. That's volatile too, but since it's all heading up, why should you care? Most investors are not concerned about risk on the upside; they are only worried about risk to the downside.

You want to be sure to protect the downside of risk, but you only have to focus on big market moves. In other words, a little bit of movement here or there shouldn't be a big deal. It's the gigantic moves that can be worrisome, so you need to be ready for those.

Dollar Cost Averaging: A Strategy for All Markets

We've talked about how to invest during the different market conditions. But there's actually a strategy that will work for almost *every* market condition: *dollar cost averaging*. Traditionally, dollar cost averaging means investing on a regular basis—for example, monthly, bimonthly, quarterly—with the same amount of money each time.

Many investors do this by having money deducted automatically from one of their bank accounts and invested on a regular basis in some ETF, mutual fund, or stock of their choice. That way, it doesn't matter whether the market is up or down, because those automatic investments will average out over time. In other words, sometimes you'll be buying when prices are high, but at other times you'll be buying when prices are low, and it will all even out in the end.

Another type of dollar cost averaging is what we call *position building*. For example, you might say to yourself, "Okay, I like this stock, or I like that sector, and I want to move into it." (Or if you're already investing in that position, you may decide to add to it.) You want to start investing in the stock or sector because you believe the conditions are appropriate. It's a good idea to first decide what percentage of your portfolio a particular investment will occupy. Perhaps you want to have 5 percent or 10 percent of your portfolio invested in that ETF or mutual fund or stock. However, instead of investing all at once to achieve that percentage, you should start off with maybe half your targeted position—for example, 2 percent or 5 percent. That way, you don't invest all at once, but instead you add to your investment as it moves in the direction you projected. This gives you the ability to confirm whether or not you made the right move. You invest a small amount and then add to it over time. How much time depends on what the conditions are: you could add to it in a day, a week, or a year, or by a specific indicator or price level.

For example, suppose you have $100,000 in your portfolio. You might invest $2,500 of that in an S&P 500 index ETF today; then next month (or above a price resistance point), you might put in another $2,500 if the condition holds. This eliminates your having to worry about when to invest. With dollar cost averaging, you're investing regularly. That's a big help for many investors, because then they don't have to worry that "Oh, my gosh, the market is up today," or "Oh, no, the market is down today; what should I do?" When you're investing regularly and automatically, you're in the game. Maybe you're not making the profits you could make with a different approach to investing, but you know that if you make a mistake, you're probably not going to lose a heap either.

The Bottom Line

Instead of thinking of the stock market as some big, nebulous thing that goes up and down randomly, think of it as being tied to the economy, which itself goes through cycles of ups and downs. It is helpful to think of the stock market as being part of one of three types of trends: uptrend for a bull market during an economic expansion, downtrend for a bear market during an economic contraction, or sideways for a transition phase during a peak or trough in the economic cycle. Just remember that not all sideways markets result in a total change in trend from bull to bear or vice versa.

During a rising stock market and booming economy, you should be concentrating your investments in the stock market but still be diversified across a variety of vehicles. These include individual stocks, sector ETFs, or broader ETFs (including index ETFs like DIA, SPY, or QQQQ) and mutual funds. Continue to do your homework, but realize that "a rising tide lifts all ships," and so you don't want to miss out on a steady uptrend. Keep up-to-date with major news events and economic reports (such as retail sales, industrial production, home sales, unemployment, and GDP) to make sure that the economic indicators are showing a rising trend as well. (You'll remember we talked about all of those reports in chapter 4.) Make sure you buy stocks that are in steady visual up trends and that exceed the fifty-day and two hundred-day moving averages on a basic stock chart.

Be on the lookout for stocks and the indexes that transition to a sideways market. This doesn't mean you should rush out and sell all of your portfolio, but you should be more selective and or defensive. Consider hedging tactics such as inverse ETFs, and pay closer attention to researching fundamentals on companies. Some stocks do well in a sideways market, while others won't do as well. Avoid stocks that break under the fifty- and two hundred-day moving averages or start to show red flags in their regular reports or earnings announcements. Keep up-to-date with news that affects the broader sectors such as technology, financial companies, industrials, materials, and health care. Certain news events can help or hurt stocks in a certain sector, and during a sideways market, you need to pay closer attention to these news items, good and bad. Also keep a closer watch on economic reports for signs of deterioration or early signs of weakness, such as a decline in consumer sentiment, retail sales, new home starts or permits, or declines in industrial production or capacity utilization. There are both opportunities and risks in a sideways market, so don't run for the hills when the trend starts to pause and stays within a certain percentage range for months on end.

Finally, if you start to see the broader indexes and index ETFs break under the fifty-day and two hundred-day moving averages, or you start to see month-to-month declines in major economic reports, then realize that we could be in, or about to turn into, a bear market correction, which will also demand your attention. Most investors do not want to hold stocks when they suspect, or their analysis tells them, that the economy might be in for some trouble ahead (as revealed through monthly economic reports, as described in chapter 4). Consider selling stocks that decline more than 10 percent or break below the two hundred-day moving average to protect yourself from even larger losses. Consider adding more bonds to your portfolio or bond ETFs for protection. Remember, the goal during a market correction is not always to make as much money as possible, but to hunker down and survive. Don't be afraid to sell mutual funds, ETFs, or stocks that are declining or showing deteriorating fundamentals. Don't get tied to a stock just because you like the name. Bear markets can devastate portfolios, and it can take a long time to recover from a sharp decline in your investments.

PART II

Analyzing Potential Investments and Monitoring Your Actual Investments

6

Determining Your
Investing Philosophy

How Do You Want to Research Possible Investments?
The Basic Difference among Quantitative,
Fundamental, and Technical Analysis

In the previous chapters we've talked about step one of investing: researching indicators to get winning ideas for what to invest in. Now it's time for step two: researching those ideas further so that you can choose specific investments and make truly informed decisions. One of the biggest challenges investors often face is the idea-generation process—that is, coming up with possible stocks to invest in. After you follow economic trends in the news, learn what's going on with particular companies and industries, and do other research, you'll have a better understanding of the investing climate and opportunities. To become a winning investor though, you'll still need to decide how you can invest accordingly.

In this chapter, I'll present an overview of the three ways to check out potential investments and decide if they're worth investing in after all.

You'll select and evaluate potential investments through

quantitative analysis, fundamental analysis, and technical analysis. Each of these approaches will be discussed in more detail in later chapters, but here you will learn the basic differences among them. Bear in mind that you don't have to choose among these three ways of analyzing investments; instead, it's best to use all three. I believe you should begin the process with quantitative analysis, then do fundamental analysis, and finally apply technical analysis. These methods are best used in combination rather than in isolation. Think of them as components of a fabulous meal—you would probably enjoy eating the meal a lot more than the individual ingredients. Or think of using all these approaches as analogous to treating some disease with a combination of surgery, medicine, and a holistic treatment.

In chapter 1, I suggested you consider how much time and energy you want to spend on your investment portfolio. With analysis, time is a factor too, because the approach you take may depend on how much time you wish to spend analyzing potential investments. In essence, the approach you choose will depend on how much time, energy, intellect, and emotion you want to put into research and analysis.

An Overview of Quantitative Analysis

Quantitative analysis is an approach to assessing investments that uses filters and screens to easily narrow down the huge list of available investments to those you want to invest in. If your research has led you to consider investing in retail stocks, you'll still need to figure out which retail stocks to choose. A *filter* is simply a set of criteria that investors can develop and use to help them narrow down the possible investments they might want to research further. A *screen* is another way to use your own criteria to narrow down possible investments. For example, you might want to look at retail companies listed in the S&P 500 index only. This type of analysis takes emotions—and even some thinking—out of the investing process so that you, the investor, do not become biased in any way about what you're investing in.

Pure quantitative analysts believe that actively managing your investments with technical or fundamental analysis (or any combination of the two) is a complete waste of time. Instead, they prefer having a computerized system choose their stocks or other investments, in order to eliminate human emotions and thought processes, which can easily complicate how and when people choose, buy, and sell their investments.

Investing exclusively with a quantitative system probably requires the least amount of time because it's completely unemotional: you simply adopt a strategy and pretty much let it run on its own. This type of analysis is almost automatic; you don't let yourself think too much about what to invest in or when to invest.

An Overview of Fundamental Analysis

Fundamental analysis, which deals with determining the value of an investment, is probably one of the most complex and time-consuming ways to evaluate investments because there are so many components you need to track. Fundamental analysts don't necessarily care what the current price of an investment is because they believe in its underlying value. In order to calculate a company's underlying value, fundamental analysts look at a slew of information, and data points, much of it from the companies themselves in the forms of quarterly reports. These reports include the following:

+ **Balance sheet**: A balance sheet shows all of a company's assets and liabilities; it's like a snapshot of a company's financial condition.

+ **Income statement**: An income statement shows a company's financial performance during a specific time frame. The typical accounting period is three months (aka a quarter because it's a quarter of a year). The income statement shows the company's net profit or loss during that time.

+ **Cash flow statement**: A cash flow statement is a report that all public companies (companies that sell stock to the public) must create for their shareholders quarterly. As the name states, this report shows how much cash is flowing in and out of the company. This is different from the snapshot of assets and liabilities shown on the balance sheet, because the cash flow statement reveals a company's short-term viability and its ability to pay its bills.

A quarterly report provides a good amount of information about a company's profitability, but because it is released only every three months, it often does not give an up-to-date picture of the company. After all, if a company has been doing well and you're looking only at the fundamentals, you might not have any idea that its earnings are suddenly plummeting. For that type of information, you have to look at a company's stock price, which will indicate what other investors are currently thinking about the stock and outlook of that company. All of the hidden voices of the market will quickly reveal either that "there's something wrong with this stock" or "there's something really right about this stock." You can see the truth in its price well before you might actually see the quarterly reports. (Note: This is where technical analysis, which we'll get to, comes in handy.)

Another challenge in using fundamental analysis is that the companies you are trying to analyze may be using very high priced accounting firms and employing savvy chief financial officers (CFOs), both of whom are trying to present their financial data in the best possible light. If you don't have the ability—and most average investors don't—to figure out every financial detail about every single company, then you might not be able to assess how well the company is really doing. Think of Enron, the energy company that deliberately misled its employees and investors before declaring bankruptcy and causing its shareholders to lose billions of dollars.

Although fundamental analysis can be hard, there's a quick and dirty way to make it easier, and that's by looking at certain ratios that offer information about a company's profitability. These ratios (which will be described in more detail in chapter 8) provide a snapshot view at a company's fundamentals. Any part or parts of the fundamentals can be put together in some type of ratio or relative number. You can calculate the ratios yourself, but they also come prepackaged and can be found on any money or financial Web site (for example, Yahoo! Finance at finance.yahoo.com, finviz.com, and many others). These ratios offer key information about a stock's value and are a quick and dirty way of taking a look at the fundamentals of a company. When you're deciding which stocks to buy, you can compare these ratios and see which ones may provide better profit opportunities.

One thing to realize about fundamental analysis is that your perception of a stock's value may not match its price. A company you've determined has a strong value may drop in price. On the other hand, many fundamental analysts like to buy stocks whose price is lower than its fundamental value, the theory being the stock price will eventually catch up with its value.

I believe investors should marry fundamental analysis with technical analysis, which is what we'll discuss next.

An Overview of Technical Analysis

Technical analysis uses charts based on an investment's price—and only on its price—to indicate patterns that can help you decide when to buy and when to sell an investment. It's used primarily for tracking the prices of stocks, although in theory it could be applied to any type of investment. Technical analysts believe that price is the only thing that pays, or matters, and that the true underlying fundamental value of an investment doesn't always determine the price. A main principle of technical analysis states that all information that can be known, and some things that are unknown to the general public, are already factored into the price of a stock.

For example, suppose you find a company with great management, an excellent track record, terrific products, exciting marketing, and on top of all that, it is very profitable. Despite all these positives, the market may not agree with your assessment and may not recognize all of a company's great attributes, and so the stock price may be low—at least lower than you believe it should be. The market may be factoring in projections about the future profitability of the company, or hidden troubles, that you won't be able to read in a historical company report. Conversely, a company could have terrible management and a terrible product, but its stock could be way up. This was true during the dot-com bubble in 1999 and 2000, when the share price of brand-new technology companies with no earnings and high debt ratios rose to values in the hundreds of dollars, while prices of stable, fundamentally sound blue-chip companies like Walmart (WMT) stayed relatively flat. What this illustrates is that sometimes stock prices can rise or fall well beyond what fundamental analysis alone would state they should be worth. Stocks rise and fall in part because of what people believe they're worth now or will be worth in the future, rather than what they're worth right now from a fundamental analysis standpoint.

To use a car analogy, technical analysts don't necessarily want to look under the hood or know anything about how the car operates. All they really appreciate is how much the car costs and how fast it goes. A well-trained technical analyst can understand a stock's potential simply by looking at charts and understanding price trends.

Another way to look at the price-versus-value debate is to think about stock as a tangible item you're trying to buy and sell, such as your house. You might say, "My house is worth a million dollars," because that's what you paid for it, or because you renovated it with high-quality materials, or because it's in a fabulous location. But if nobody wants to buy your house for $1 million, then it's really not worth $1 million, even though you paid that amount for it. It doesn't matter if your house is made of gold if nobody is willing to pay the price. Your house is only worth what a buyer will actually pay. That's why technical analysts only care about price.

Technical analysis often requires less time than other types of analysis because you don't actually need to pore over and study a company (or investment) itself. Instead, you need to watch only the chart price trend which reveals whether the market of investors who are currently buying and selling have already decided if a stock should move higher or lower. Technical analysis says it doesn't matter if the company is loaded with debt, the president just quit, or the company is going bankrupt; if the stock price is going higher, that's all that matters, until the trend changes. And looking at the price is certainly much easier than monitoring a company's ratios and reports, and focusing on how the overall sector is doing.

Another benefit of technical analysis is that it's graphical and visual, so it's easier to track price trends. Many investors prefer technical analysis because it relies on charting as the best way to understand the past trend of an investment, and charting gives you much more immediate and timely information than fundamental analysis. For instance, the company report you might be looking at now may have been released last quarter, and it was probably more than a month old by the time you started reading it. Stock charts also give you a much better indication of where things might be in the mind of the market, which is all that really matters. Remember, the market is like the customer; it's always right.

All of this is not to say that technical analysis is a walk in the park: studying charts can be a lot of work. No analysis is easy, but most individual investors prefer technical analysis because it's much more efficient: you simply track the price trends and indicators, and if they move one way, you buy; if they move another way, you sell. As mentioned, there are many indicators you can monitor, which are beyond the scope of this book.*

Let's take a look at a few examples to illustrate why technical analysis often trumps fundamental analysis. There's a company called AutoNation (AN), which is a new and used car dealer. During the summer of 2009, major car companies such as General Motors and Chrysler filed for bankruptcy. You may have thought all car dealers were doing terribly, and a fundamental analyst may have concluded that the car industry was not doing so hot. With that knowledge, you would not have considered investing in this type of company's stock. But astonishingly, at that time the stock price of AutoNation was approaching a five-year high, showing that price trumps fundamentals.

Similarly, many investors thought the earnings outlook for

---

*Again, see Brian Shannon's *Technical Analysis Using Multiple Timeframes*.

the retail sector was terrible throughout 2008–2009. Unemployment was up, and both consumer sentiment and consumer spending were down. Most believed that retailers were hard pressed to make money. Yet Abercrombie & Fitch (ANF) and certain other companies in the retail sector were on fire as their stock price rose month over month despite the seemingly poor fundamental economic environment.

Those are just two examples of how technical analysis can sometimes provide information that current economic reports, quarterly reports, balance sheets, or other forms of fundamental analysis cannot.

On the other hand, be sure to keep in mind what your research shows, because even if the technicals (charts) show something different, if the future of a company is questionable, its stock price will eventually reflect that. As mentioned, the sky-high prices of technology companies in 1999 and 2000 soared on very poor fundamentals. All of those high-flying prices eventually crashed down, with many stocks falling 80 percent or more. Reality does catch up; pundits have long said that stocks and markets can stay irrational longer than an investor can stay solvent—assuming he or she battles the trend. It's best to find fundamentally sound companies in uptrends, which gives a more complete picture than either form of analysis can do alone.

The quick and dirty tip to remember is that in certain market conditions, the market and stock prices may not make sense, and so you need to use technical analysis to evaluate the investment environment. Even if you prefer to use fundamental analysis as your primary investing philosophy, remember that over time one of two things are going to happen. First, the pricing target based on well-researched fundamental analysis should eventually meet your technical-analysis price projection. And second, over time the technicals may catch up to the fundamentals, causing the price to revert to "normality," which is exactly what happened during the dot-com boom and bust.

Using a Mix of Quantitative, Fundamental, and Technical Analysis

As mentioned earlier, you don't have to choose only one type of analysis. My investment firm uses multiple approaches to come up with our own investing ideas and actions. We find this helpful because it provides a system of checks and balances—in other words, we don't rely on only one type of analysis. We use quantitative analysis as a screening process for idea generation, to provide ideas for what we might want to invest in. Sometimes we also come up with possible investment ideas via the "Peter Lynch way": we walk into a store and see what is selling wildly, or we do research on what seems like a great product—for example, the iPhone by Apple (AAPL). Peter Lynch* thought that watching consumer trends was a great way to discover profitable investment ideas.

When you're searching for a stock idea, you have to figure out where to begin. As investment advisors, we start with quantitative analysis (which we'll discuss in detail in chapter 7). Then once we compile our final list of investments to research further—whether it's a list of stocks based on a certain fundamental or technical screen, or stocks from a specific sector or industry—then we can start looking at the fundamentals. It's important to understand that the fundamentals can carry a stock over the longer term. As

---

*Peter Lynch is a Wall Street investor who has spent most of his career at Fidelity Investments; he is also the author of three investing books (*One Up on Wall Street, Beating the Street,* and *Learn to Earn*). One of his most famous investment strategies is "Invest in what you know."

we've seen with such examples as the dot-com bubble, the banking crisis, and Enron, without the core fundamentals, there's a chance you could get caught holding the bag if all the shareholders believe that a stock is overvalued, and its price starts moving down. There's often a crowded rush for the exit once the investors realize that a company's share price is headed for a sharply lower path. On the other hand, by looking at the fundamentals and then projecting out into the future, we can sometimes find stocks that may be *undervalued*.

Once we understand the fundamentals of an investment we're considering investing in, then we study the technicals/charts to figure out at what price point we may want to initiate a purchase of the stock (or a sale of the stock, if it's one we have already invested in). Technical analysis gives us insight into what the consensus is—that is, what other investors believe a stock is valued at—at any given time.

Combining these three different approaches gives us the added benefit of a system of checks and balances as we consider whether to buy or hold a position or eventually sell. All too often, investors end up falling in love with a stock. They say, "Oh, I love this company," or "I inherited this stock from my parents," or "Someone I trust gave me a tip about this company's stock." Without a system or process, these investors never know exactly when to sell, because they're not evaluating the investment unemotionally. However, by using one or all of these approaches—quantitative, fundamental, and technical analysis—you have a dedicated *system* to help you decide what and when to buy, hold, and sell. If you note a significant change in the fundamentals—maybe earnings are slowing down for a company, maybe the company has high debt load, or maybe there's even a significant management change—you may rethink whether you want to continue to hold on to your investment. It's a lot safer than saying, "Well, I really like the stock, and

I'm going to hold on to it forever." If you commit to holding a stock forever, you need to realize that a lot of things can happen: the price may go up and up and up, or it may stay stagnant, or the company may even go bankrupt. However, if you don't have a system to help you decide whether an investment is still worthwhile, then you're never going to do anything with it. That approach *could* serve you well over the long term. However, as discussed in chapter 1, this approach is also called passive investing, or lazy investing, or Sleeping Beauty investing, and there have been plenty of times in history when investing this way has been a very unprofitable experience.

Finally, there are Web sites, such as Barchart.com, that provide indicators that suggest when it's time to buy or sell particular stocks. In addition, finviz.com, Google Finance, among others have "quant" screeners that you can use to generate ideas. As mentioned previously, however, such screeners typically help with quantitative analysis so you can find ideas for investments to investigate further. But you still need to make sure your ideas check out, using either fundamental or technical analysis, or both. Before we get into the details of those approaches, we'll take a closer look at the first step, quantitative analysis.

7

Quantitative Analysis

Investing without Emotion

As mentioned in chapter 6, quantitative analysis uses screens/ filters to help you find a list of stocks (or other type of invest- ments) that meet certain criteria that you've predefined. Essentially, it's a way to generate ideas for what you might want to invest in, and it has many benefits. For one, it's another way to prevent emo- tion from getting in the way of your decision-making process, avoiding fear of loss and greed of gains. You use filters, screens, and searches based on historical facts instead of any preconceived ideas you may have about a stock, based on its name, industry, sec- tor, or even the location of the company's corporate offices. These biases can often subconsciously convince you to buy or not buy. Quantitative analysis prevents you from not buying Starbucks (SBUX), for example, because you don't like their coffee, even if you find that the company is doing well. Another benefit to using quantitative analysis is that it can introduce you to companies you've never heard of. If I were to ask you, "What does Bucyrus (BUCY) do?" you probably wouldn't know. Bucyrus, which makes mining equipment, might be a good company to invest in. But if you've never heard of it, then you can't research it to find out more.

Quantitative analysis has many benefits. This chapter will introduce you to some of the tools of quantitative analysis and will show you how you can best use them to make winning investment decisions.

Quantitative Analysis Helps You Generate Ideas

We've already discussed why it's important to diversify your portfolio by investing in indexes through mutual funds and/or ETFs. However, it's also important to invest in individual stocks. There's a big difference between just investing your money in an ETF that tracks the S&P 500 index—or any other index fund—versus investing in individual stocks. Generally when you're investing in ETFs or mutual funds, your investments are simply moving in the same direction as the market, rising and falling as the tide of the market ebbs and flows. When the stock market as a whole is up, you're up; when it's down, you're down. When you invest in individual stocks though, you can do well even if the overall market isn't doing so well. The reverse is also true: your stocks may be falling sharply in price, while the rest of the market is booming. So since an individual stock may go up or down independent of what the market is doing, it's a good idea to hold some individual stocks in your portfolio.

People ask me all the time where I get ideas for stocks to invest in. Well, quantitative analysis is often the first method I use to help me find companies and stocks to invest in. The first step in quantitative analysis is to come up with criteria for the stocks I want to invest in. These criteria will be used to create the screens that will then uncover the stocks that meet my requirements. Of course, my criteria will differ from any other investor's criteria. I may want to consider large-cap retail companies only; others may want utility company stocks only; then there are others that may be open to stocks in any sector but may want to invest only in stocks priced under $10.

In order to come up with your criteria, think about the kinds of companies you want to invest in. Think of it like dating. Your criteria for who you're looking for will be different than someone else's. One person prefers to meet a brunette under five foot eight with a good sense of humor, whereas another person wants someone from the West Coast who is adventuresome, loves the outdoors, and speaks more than one language. Some people, just like some investors, are more picky than others, and that's fine. The bottom line is that there are all kinds of parameters you can set.

Here's an example. Anita has a mutual fund managed by someone else. She recently got a promotion and now has more money to put toward investing. She wants to invest in stocks but is only interested in those from companies that meet the following criteria:

- stocks priced at more than $10 a share
- stocks that are part of the S&P 500 index
- companies whose market capitalization* is more than $1 billion
- companies whose earnings are growing by 20 percent each year
- companies that have debt ratios below 25 percent

---

*Recall that market capitalization is a measure of a company's size, in terms of the number of outstanding shares multiplied by the price—for example, if Starbucks has 10 million shares outstanding, and its current stock price is $23, then its market cap is $230 million. See chapter 2 for more info.

✦ companies whose sales have increased by at least 10 percent in each quarter over the past two years

When Anita uses these criteria in our hypothetical example, twenty-five stocks pop up. At this point, she has a few options. She can simply invest in all of those stocks, tweak the filter further, or she can go beyond quantitative analysis to look at the fundamentals and then the technicals (charts) of each stock individually. As discussed in chapter 6, I believe quantitative analysis is just the first step in researching investments; fundamental analysis is the second step; technical analysis is the third and final step before purchasing a stock; and the three approaches are best used in combination instead of isolation. Quantitative analysis generates a list of stocks for you, fundamental analysis filters out the best companies in that list, and technical analysis serves as a final check on the stocks that remain. The simple formula is to find stocks that are screened to your criteria, fundamentally sound, and in a stable rising uptrend on their price charts.

How to Create Stock Screens

There are a number of different Web sites that you can use to create stock screens and to get ideas for what criteria to use. Try the Google Finance pages, Yahoo!, FINVIZ (finviz.com), and other popular sites. Try to balance your scan criteria so that they're not too simple (too many results) and not too complex or strict (too few companies). Try the precanned screens at one of the sites I just mentioned to get a feel for what they're all about. Play around with these tools to see which stocks come up in the scans you select. Remember, you should never run out and buy a stock just because it comes up on a screen you run. That's not a winning strategy. If it were that easy, there'd be no need for fundamental or technical analysis at all!

In addition to using criteria that you devise yourself, you can also use other quantitative screens and strategies. Let's take a closer at two of them: the Dogs of the Dow and GARP.

Using the Dogs of the Dow to Screen for Potential Investments

The Dogs of the Dow approach to investing is a technique that has been used for years: it screens for the 10 highest dividend-yielding companies from the 30 within the Dow Jones Industrial Average (DJIA).* Typically, you would screen for these top 10 stocks toward the end of the calendar year—say, in late November or December— and once you'd identified them, you'd invest the same amount of money in each of them. Now, that's a very easy way to use quantitative analysis, but before you go off and do this, let me explain the thinking behind this strategy.

To explain the Dogs of the Dow strategy, we need to first explain what a high dividend-yielding stock is. To do so, let's take a look at Company X2. Company X2's stock is priced at $10 a share, and it pays $0.50 a share in dividends. To calculate its dividend rate, we divide the dividend amount per share by the share price ($0.50/$10), which is 5 percent; therefore, its dividend rate is 5 percent. Suppose Company X2's stock price then plummets to $5 per share, so it's now worth only half of what it used to be worth. Though the price drops, it's still paying $0.50 per share. The actual dividend amount hasn't changed, but the percentage yield has. It's now paying a 10 percent yield per share (because $0.50 divided by $5 is 10 percent). The ten stocks that have the highest dividend

---

*Recall from chapter 2 that the Dow Industrials are some of the largest companies that offer stock to the public, and that a dividend is a share of profits, which public companies (i.e., companies that offer stock to the public) pay to their shareholders.

yield (that is, the dividend amount divided by the stock price) are the Dogs of the Dow. The name is based on the saying "Every dog has its day," suggesting that stocks that were "beat up" the most last year will be some of the rising names this year, or at least will outperform the stocks that were not as beaten down.

This investing strategy has you looking for the dividend stocks whose prices have performed the worst—and perhaps plummeted the most—during the preceding calendar year. If you can find those stocks, not only do you get a decent dividend from them, but because compared to the other twenty stocks in the Dow that performed better, many of these ten underperforming stocks will have been sold off—and so there may be an opportunity for them to turn around and recover prior losses, so the theory goes. When you invest in the Dogs of the Dow, you're not buying the hot, hot, hot companies; you're buying the companies that are ice cold. The thinking is contrarian—that these stocks have nowhere to go but up, so you may be able to profit from those investments. A contrarian investor does the opposite of what other investors are doing: buying when others are selling or selling while others are buying. As mentioned earlier, the Dogs of the Dow screen toward the end of the year. You purchase the ten stocks on January 1, and then hold them for one year. At the end of the year, you sell your positions in the old Dogs (whether or not you made or lost money), and you start all over again to find the *new* Dogs— the new top ten highest-yielding dividend stocks, which have probably changed since the previous year.

This strategy is not guaranteed to work. One main problem with it is that over the years the composition of the DJIA has changed, and some of the companies do not pay any dividends. If fewer companies among the thirty within the DJIA pay dividends, you don't really have thirty stocks to choose from, which cuts down on your opportunity to find stocks that will work with this strategy.

As mentioned earlier, when you're selecting from a number of stocks using a quantitative screen, it is better when you have more stocks to choose from. The top ten of a list of twenty-five stocks is not as broad a pool as the top ten stocks from a list of hundred or more.

In addition, there's no guarantee that a stock will reverse its trend and suddenly start trading higher just because it was beaten down the year before. A stock down 10 percent might go on to be down 20 percent, and then fall further to lose 30 percent, and so on. Some of the losing stocks of last year will be the losing stocks of this year and will not turn around. Remember, we don't buy a stock just because it seems cheap. The Dogs of the Dow strategy has an additional advantage in that it considers dividend yield in addition to price.

Still, the Dogs of the Dow have proven over time to be a good strategy. They may not be profitable every year, but historically the Dogs have outperformed the Dow. In his book *What Works on Wall Street*, James P. O'Shaughnessy researched seventy-five years of results—from December 1928 through December 2003—to compare the performance of the Dogs of the Dow against other stock indexes and quant strategies. He found the Dogs returned an average of 14.3 percent per year, and therefore the Dogs outperformed the thirty companies included in the DJIA, which returned only 11.7 percent on average during that period. For more information on the Dogs of the Dow, check out www.dogsofthedow.com.

Now let's take a look at another quantitative analysis screen you might want to consider.

Using GARP to Screen for Potential Investment Opportunities

Screening for stocks that offer growth at a reasonable price is another way to search for potential investments using quantitative analysis. *Growth at a reasonable price* (GARP) is a strategy that combines both growth investing and value investing to locate individual stocks to buy. Those using this strategy would look for companies with steady growth in earnings that are above broad market levels, but they would also exclude companies that have high valuations. This strategy seeks first to avoid the extreme of growth—that is buying stocks at P/E ratios (discussed in chapter 8) that are too high and thus the share price is deemed too expensive (this can happen with popular "trendy" stocks). And it also seeks to avoid the extreme of value, buying a stock just because it is cheap (and not because it has fundamental value). The GARP method is a hybrid between (1) investing in growth stocks, which are earnings-based stocks whose future earnings are expected to grow faster than those of other stocks in the market and yield above-average returns as the company grows, and (2) investing in value stocks, which are established stocks that trade at a discounted price or lower value than their fundamental valuation indicates (using ratios and fundamental analysis).

GARP is sort of the halfway point between these two types of strategies. The GARP approach focuses on finding opportunities that have a modest risk, within the realm of smaller-capitalization stocks. This approach might identify stocks that have either fallen from grace in the eyes of investors or that have simply never caught fire; nevertheless, these companies are still growing. Specifically, a GARP investor would look to buy stocks with a price-to-earnings growth (PEG) ratio of 1 or less. The PEG ratio shows the ratio between a company's P/E (or price-to-earnings) ratio and the expected growth rate of the next few years. We'll discuss these ratios in more detail in the next chapter. Just look at GARP as the best of both worlds when it comes to value and growth investing. It combines the best parts of both strategies to uncover stocks that are undervalued relative to their peers, but may have good future growth potential. As a broad generalization, growth investors want the share price of the company to grow as much as possible (and they don't mind overpaying for a stock), while value investors want to buy stocks that are the most undervalued bargains and hold them for a long time until their share price rises. Growth investors often have a shorter time horizon than value investors. The GARP strategy seeks to find stocks that might be seen as "too slow growing" by growth investors but that perhaps are not as cheap (relative to other stocks) as a value investor might like.

Always make a distinction between *value* and *cheap*. Never buy a stock just because it is cheap. Instead, always compare it to similar companies in its sector and industry, evaluating P/E ratio, price, market cap, and other factors we'll discuss later.

A GARP scan might include limiting your universe of stocks to those with a market cap under $1 billion and with a PEG ratio equal to or less than 1.* To narrow your results, include filters that scan for as high as possible an EPS (earnings per share) growth projection over the next five years and for five-year projected revenue growth, also as high as possible. GARP is used by many investment managers, as it is halfway between go-go growth and value investing.

Now that you know a little about the theory behind quantitative analysis, let's look at the next approach to researching investments: fundamental analysis. Once you've used quantitative analysis to see what investments may be candidates for your portfolio, you should move to the fundamentals of those companies to see if they're really worth investing in.

---

*If you're interested in creating screens that will uncover GARP stocks, comprehensive details on how to do this (and other strategies) are provided in my previous book, *The Disciplined Investor: Essential Strategies for Success*.

8

Fundamental Analysis: It's All about *Value*, Not Price

How to Do the Math

After you've used quantitative analysis to identify stocks you may want to invest in, you can then employ fundamental analysis to further research these stocks. Of course, you can also use fundamental analysis to monitor the stocks you already own to see whether you want to keep or sell them.

As mentioned in chapter 6, a key component of fundamental analysis is looking at various ratios. Ratios are indicators that give investors valuable information about much bigger issues with the company whose stock they're evaluating. True fundamental analysts dig deeper and look at more than just ratios, but because we're all about the quick and dirty way to do things, we'll focus primarily on these ratios. Ratios are useful because they can give you important information you need to assess a company's financials, and they provide a relatively easy way to compare the stocks of different companies.

In this chapter I'll give you tips on which ratios you might want to look at and what they tell you about a company. I'll define and describe simple ratios used for evaluating stocks so you will know how to use them to make sensible investing decisions. There are dozens and dozens of fundamental data points that you could look at, but the ratios described in this chapter are the primary ones that most investors use to evaluate potential winning investments. Also keep in mind that you should look at all of these ratios, not just one or two in isolation. As you learn more about whatever you're considering investing in, you're more likely to make better investing decisions. In other words, you shouldn't just look at one particular ratio of a stock and decide, "Okay, that's something I want to buy now." Instead, you need to look at a number of ratios, many of which will be described in this chapter. Though you can find ratios for companies on numerous financial Web sites, I'm also going to tell you how to calculate them yourself; this will help you understand what they are and what they represent.

Earnings-per-Share (EPS) Ratio

Earnings–per–share ratio (EPS) is the net earnings, or income, of a company, divided by the number of shares of stock that are outstanding. Outstanding shares are those shares that are currently held by investors, including restricted shares owned by the company's officers and insiders, as well as those held by the public, but not including shares that have been repurchased by the company. In other words:

$$EPS = net\ income \div shares\ outstanding$$

Calculating a company's earnings per share (EPS) is one of the clearest ways to understand whether or not that company is profitable. Here's a sample calculation: suppose a company has

2 million shares outstanding, and the company's annual income is
$4 million. This company's EPS is:

$$EPS = \$4 \text{ million net income} \div 2 \text{ million shares}$$

Therefore, the company's EPS = $2.

You can find a company's earnings in its annual report, on its
Web site, or on any money Web site, such as Yahoo! Finance,
Bloomberg, Google Finance, and FINVIZ. And to make things
even easier, you don't even have to calculate a company's EPS
yourself, because you can find the EPS listed on almost any investing Web site. For example, go to www.msnmoney.com, type
in "Apple," and a list of companies will come up—everything from
Apple Inc. (the one we're looking for, which makes the Macs and
iPhones) to Apple Orthodontix. Once you choose the right Apple,
the site provides you the stock symbol, which is AAPL, and once
you click on that, you'll see a list of ratios on the right-hand side of
the page.

For most fundamental analysts and investors, earnings are
the most important component for calculating the true value of a
stock. Keep in mind that historical earnings information is easy
to find; unfortunately, future earnings are more difficult to estimate.
Obviously, looking at past success is not the best way to assess how
well a company will do in the future.

Price-to-Earnings (P/E) Ratio

Another good ratio to analyze when evaluating a stock is a company's *price-to-earnings (P/E) ratio*. The P/E ratio is a calculation of
a company's stock price (P) divided by that company's earnings per
share (E), which we just calculated. P/E ratio tells you how much
investors are willing to pay for the stock, as compared to that com-

pany's earnings. The P/E ratio is important because it's not enough to look at the current price of a stock and determine how expensive it really is.

Let's do a sample calculation for the P/E ratio of Apple (AAPL). Say the stock price is $172.17, and the EPS is $5.72.

$$\$172.17 \div \$5.72 = 30.09$$

In this example, you're paying thirty times the earnings for the stock, or, as investors say, "a thirty multiple."

Why does this matter? How does this information help you? Well, you have to determine the value of a business somehow, and one way to do so is to value the stream of income the company will produce. The more income the company produces, the more valuable the company is (at least in terms of net income).

A P/E ratio is also useful because it can tell you whether a stock is overvalued or undervalued. In a nutshell, the P/E ratio provides a good idea of the relative value of a stock when compared to its competitors. Once you've calculated a company's P/E ratio, you need to evaluate what the ratio tells you. In other words, is this company's P/E ratio too high or too low, as compared to its peer group? We use P/E ratios for comparison, because there is no one number or range of numbers that determines a good or bad P/E ratio. P/E ratios aren't like cholesterol levels, where any number under 200 is good, but 200 or over is cause for concern. It's a relative number, not an absolute. In other words, there's no benchmark for P/E ratios.

To understand how to evaluate a company's P/E ratio, let's look at an actual example, using Dell (DELL). If you go to MSN's www.moneycentral.msn.com and type in "Dell" in the blank field next to "Get Quote," the site takes you to a page where you'll find the P/E ratio for Dell. Let's say it's 18.

What can we make of this information? The answer brings me to another point: in order to truly evaluate a P/E ratio, you have to compare it to the P/E ratio of other companies in the same industry. Traditionally, Dell was a technology stock, but today we can debate whether it's a technology stock or a retail stock. Dell does build computers, but that manufacturing has really become commoditized, or largely automated. Today Dell is best known for selling computers either online or through retail stores, not for its innovation in the field of technology like Apple Computers, Microsoft, or other big technology companies would be. Yes, Apple Inc. sells computers through retail stores, but it also continues to make innovative new products like the iPhone, iPad, and iPod.

For the reasons just mentioned, Dell Inc. can be considered a hybrid between technology and retail. In that respect, Dell Inc. is more similar to a company like Best Buy (BBY) or Amazon.com (AMZN), because it sells many different products. If you look at www.dell.com, you'll see that the company also sells televisions, printers, ink cartridges, mobile phones, digital cameras, software, and even backpacks. But none of these items were necessarily invented or built by Dell in its factories.

In order to evaluate Dell's P/E ratio and put it in context, we need to compare it to the P/E ratio of other technology and retail hybrids, such as Best Buy and Amazon. Comparing Dell with at least a few other companies of its kind is important, because different companies within different sectors and different industries will have different P/E ratios. Most investors will be willing to pay more for innovative technology companies with big growth opportunities, so the P/Es of tech companies are usually going to be a lot higher—in the 20s, 30s, or even 40s. In contrast, because a utility company is a much more stable, steady, value-oriented investment, its P/E will usually be a lot lower. In addition, companies in the technology sector have P/E ratios that are usually much higher than those of companies in the health-care industry, which are also considered to be more stable.

The bottom line is that the P/E ratio is helpful, but it should be viewed only as a comparative ratio, comparing one company against another (within the same industry). You need to compare apples to apples, so you can determine how Dell really stacks up against its competitors, how expensive its stock is, and if, in fact, there is an aberration in its stock price.

On the date I'm writing this, the P/E ratio of a few other technology companies are as follows:

+ Dell's P/E is 12.1.
+ Apple's P/E is 18.3.
+ Hewlett-Packard's P/E is 9.6.

From this information, it looks like Hewlett-Packard has the lowest price per earnings, making it the cheapest. Therefore, if you were looking solely at P/E ratios, Hewlett-Packard seems to be a good buy and something you might want to invest in.

However, you should also compare Dell's P/E ratio against some technology retail hybrids, such as Best Buy (BBY) or Amazon.com (AMZN). You want to make the most informed investment decision, so it helps to consider all the companies Dell might compete with. The P/E is basically a ratio to look at initially in order to compare the priciness of a company's stock to that of its competitors.

As with all ratios, it's not enough just to compare P/E ratios; P/E is only one factor you want to look at. Just like when you're buying anything, you need to consider other criteria as well. For example, when you buy clothing, you don't just consider how well it fits and what it costs but also how it looks on you and how it makes you feel. Or when you choose a college, you don't consider only the quality of the education, but also where the school is located and if that's where and how you want to live for four years, as well as how many other students are attending and whether you'll fit in with them.

Considering the P/E ratio is helpful, but if you want a much better way to look at P/E, you need to look at it in terms of growth. That's where another ratio, the PEG ratio, comes into the picture.

Quick and Dirty Tip

There's no real benchmark for P/E ratios that state something like, "Okay, if it's higher than 12, that's too expensive." However, you can use that logic when you look at a company's P/E historically— by comparing a company's P/E ratio to itself over time to see periods when its own stock has been expensive or a bargain. You don't always have to compare P/E ratios with other companies for a reference. Some advanced charting software programs allow you to plot the P/E ratio over time underneath the price bars of a chart. This shows you when the stock reached certain high or low P/E ratio numbers over time. You can also plot a one-year average of the P/E ratio to see if the stock is higher or lower than the average P/E over the last year.

Price-to-Earnings-to-Growth (PEG) Ratio

When considering investing in a company, always ask yourself, "How does the price reflect the growth of the company's earnings over time?" The answer is the company's *price-to-earnings-to-growth (PEG) ratio*. The PEG ratio is the P/E ratio divided by the company's expected per-share earnings growth over the next few years. You can find a company's estimated earnings growth on most money sites, such as Yahoo! www.yahoo.com/finance. Simply click on "Earnings Estimates" on the left side of the page, and then you'll see "Analyst Estimates," with an "average estimate" as well.

Let's do a sample calculation. If the company's earnings growth rate is 9.6, it means that analysts expect the company to grow almost 10 percent for the next 5 years. Suppose that company's P/E ratio is 11.1. Then all you need to do is divide the P/E ratio by growth:

$$P/E \text{ ratio} \div \text{expected earnings growth rate} = PEG \text{ ratio}$$

or

$$11.1 \div 9.6 = 1.1$$

That's the PEG: 1.1. Now let's put it in context. Unlike the P/E ratio whose significance you can only understand by comparing it with other P/E ratios, with the PEG ratio you get information simply based on the number:

+ A **PEG ratio over 2**: The company's stock may be a little bit more expensive than it should be, so you may wish to consider avoiding it.
+ A **PEG ratio of 1**: The company could be fairly valued because its P/E ratio, compared to its ongoing growth in the future, is right on.
+ A **PEG ratio of less than 1**: Especially if its significantly less than 1, this ratio shows that the stock price may be undervalued, because the company's earnings are projected

to be much greater than the P/E ratio and the earnings expectations into the future.

As mentioned in chapter 7, you could use quantitative analysis and create a screen that looks for PEG ratios between 0 and 1. You do a simple search for companies with a PEG ratio between 0 and 1, or greater than 2, or greater than 1, or whatever parameter you choose. Again, you can create your screens on a variety of different Web sites, including FINVIZ, Google Finance, and others. Some are free; some you have to pay for.

Price-to-Book Ratio

Another ratio you should use is a company's *price-to-book ratio*. This ratio compares a stock's current market price to its book value, which is simply the company's assets minus its liabilities. Let's break that down into its component parts:

+ **Assets**: A company's assets are what it owns. Assets typically include cash, short-term investments, accounts receivable, inventory, real estate holdings, plant and equipment, long-term investments, and goodwill, among others.
+ **Liabilities**: A company's liabilities are what it owes. Liabilities typically include short-term borrowing (i.e., debt, loans), accounts payable, dividends payable, taxes payable, long-term debt, pension obligations, and deferred taxes, among others.

To calculate the price-to-book ratio, find the latest price of the stock of the company you're interested in, and divide it by that company's book value per share during the most recent quarter. Again, you can find this information on financial Web sites.

When you're looking at a company's price-to-book ratio, you're looking at whether the company's stock is trading at a premium or at a discount when compared to the actual worth of the company. The price-to-book ratio shows how much the company would be worth if it were forced to close its doors and liquidate. The ideal price-to-book ratio is 1:1, but that's only an ideal; very rarely do you find a company with a 1:1 ratio.

A 1:1 ratio means that each share has assets backing it. The company is not simply betting on its potential; instead, there are actual assets backing your investment in the company. So when you get down to 1, you could almost say to yourself, "Wait a minute! I'm buying a company that's only trading 1 times its book value. That means that any earnings that the company makes and any deals that it does are gravy." You're more likely to find companies with price-to-book ratios higher than 1. For example, if the stock price is $10 per share, but the book value is $5, then the company is trading at 2 times its book value.

Let's look at this from a different viewpoint, in terms of something more tangible. Let's say you own a house: that's an asset. You're not going to rent it out; you're not going to do anything to it; it's just a house. Let's assume that the price of the house and the value of the house are identical. Then let's suppose that one day the house is for sale for $200,000—even though you bought it for only $100,000. You've done nothing to that house. You haven't renovated it; you haven't updated it; it's still exactly the same house you bought. Yet all of a sudden the house is "trading" (i.e., selling, or for sale) at 2 times the book value (its real value).

In other words, the higher the price-to-book ratio, the more you're getting away from the true value of the underlying asset. In this case, it's a house, but if we were talking about a stock, the underlying asset would be the value of the company whose stock you're buying. If the price-to-book value is 50, that could be rather worrisome. Suppose you built a new house that you value at $1 million, and somebody offers you $50 million. On the one hand, that's great for you, the seller, because you'll make $49 million on that deal. On the other hand, though, the underlying price-to-book is out of control, because the buyer is paying $50 million for something that's only worth $1 million. The higher the price-to-book value, the more expensive the company may be, as compared to its book value.

There's no general rule of thumb for a "good" price-to-book value. Personally, I like to look at 2 and under, depending on the company. Some companies may be asset-rich; other companies may not. For example, service companies are not asset-rich, whereas companies that sell materials are asset-rich, because they have products, materials, and inventory.

Quick and Dirty Tip

A company that has a lower price-to-book ratio than its competitors is on much more solid footing during times of difficult economic conditions. If the company needs to liquidate its assets, there are plenty of assets for it to sell if it needs to, or to use when sales slow.

Putting It All Together

You should look at all the ratios described in this chapter on a continual basis, because they will help you narrow down the myriad of investment choices. Here's how: suppose certain indicators and trends show that there is going to be a tremendous need for green energy and eco-friendly products in buildings around the world. Once you have that information, you might consider investing in companies that are involved in that business directly and indirectly. For instance, are there companies that make solar panels, silicon wafers, turbines for wind power, or any other related products or industries? If you can narrow down the industries you want to research, then you can use many of the ratios we've discussed to find the companies that meet the criteria you've established.

Let's take a look at a quick comparison. Go to the Web site www.nasdaq.com, and type in the symbol of any company in the "Get Stock Quotes" box. Then click on "View Competitors" under the "Stock Analysis" tab. The Web site then selects competitors for the company you chose, and allows you to compare quick ratios.

The following table is a replication of a chart made May 25, 2010, using Exxon-Mobil (XOM) as the input and comparing it with competitors Chevron Corporation (CVX), ConocoPhillips (COP), and British Petroleum (BP).

Stock Comparison				
Symbol	CVX	COP	BP	XOM
Company	Chevron Corp.	ConocoPhillips	British Petroleum	Exxon Mobil
Market Value	$145b	$76b	$38b	$280b
Earnings				
EPS ratio	$6.48	$4.60	$5.63	$4.46
P/E ratio	11.20	10.85	7.56	13.39
PEG ratio	1.04	0.71	1.19	0.58

Of the four companies, Chevron Corporation has the highest EPS, or earnings per share, but Exxon Mobil has the highest P/E, or price-to earnings ratio. When it comes to the PEG, or price-to-earnings-to-growth ratio, Exxon Mobil has the cheapest ratio at 0.58, while BP has the highest at just above 1.0 at 1.19. (Remember, lower than 1.0 means the price is cheaper, while higher than 1.0 means the price might be expensive.)

So what does this tell us when we need to make a decision to buy one of these stocks?

Chevron Corporation has the highest EPS value, which is the earnings divided by the number of shares outstanding, and gives us an indication of company's profitability. Investors who are interested only in earnings, and many are, would select Chevron. But does EPS give us the total picture?

Move down to the P/E ratio, which lets us know whether a stock price might be trading higher than it should be, and thus may not be a very good value. Remember, most investors want to buy low and sell high, so buying a company that has the highest EPS in a comparison might not fulfill that requirement. The P/E ratio divides the stock price by the earnings per share, which we see as the EPS number. When this table was created, Chevron traded at $72.57, Conoco Phillips at $49.92, BP at $42.56, and Exxon at $59.71. We divide these figures by the EPS for each company to normalize the share prices. At first glance, you might think Chevron is overpriced at $72.57, but you don't get the whole story from a stock's price alone. In reality, when we look at the P/E ratio, Exxon, with the second highest share price of our group, is the most expensive stock. So of the four, Exxon is the most expensive, while BP is actually the cheapest. As I write this, BP's stock has fallen sharply from its $60 price in April 2010, because of the oil spill disaster in the Gulf of Mexico. Its stock price has fallen sharply, and that is reflected in the P/E ratio as being the cheapest in the group. This is a good example of how external events can affect the stock price of an individual company in a group, even if it is in the same sector or industry group with stocks that are not affected. If you wanted to buy an undervalued stock and stay away from an expensive one, then you would look to BP instead of Exxon. BP's P/E ratio is almost half of what Exxon's is!

The final comparison is the PEG, or price-to-earnings growth, ratio. This ratio divides the P/E ratio by the expected rate of earnings growth for the future. This figure is compiled as an average number from analyst expectations, which you can find at the Web site nasdaq.com and many other financial Web sites. The PEG is a bit subjective, because we cannot know exactly how the earnings of a company will grow into the future, and so it is based on professional assumptions instead of facts (like earnings, shares outstanding, and share price). A ratio number of 1.0 means that the P/E ratio is fairly priced with respect to future earnings potential. A ratio greater than 1.0 means that the P/E ratio, and the price of the stock, might be higher than analysts forecast assuming the company will grow. A PEG ratio less than 1.0 means that the company may be underpriced by the market relative to analyst expectations of future growth. Like the P/E ratio, the lower the number, the cheaper the company is, and the higher the number, the more expensive the company is.

In our example, Exxon has the lowest PEG ratio at 0.587, while BP has the highest PEG ratio at 1.196. How can that be possible? We just said that Exxon's share price was high based on P/E ratio, and BP's was cheap. How can it be the opposite now? Again, the PEG ratio takes into account assumptions about the future, particularly what the rate of earnings growth will be over the next year or longer. At best, the analysts are making an educated guess about future earnings. In this example, we would say Chevron has a PEG ratio of 1.04, which means that the P/E ratio and price of the stock are fairly priced, given future expectations, or that it is priced correctly in line with analyst expectations. BP's PEG ratio of 1.196 means it is just slightly overpriced, and

Exxon's PEG ratio of 0.58 means it is probably underpriced relative to future growth.

So of the four, which stock should you buy? Chevron would be the choice of investors who are looking to buy a fairly priced stock that is neither too expensive nor too cheap, given that its P/E ratio is in the midpoint of our four companies and its PEG ratio was almost exactly 1.0. It also had the highest EPS at $6.48, which makes it the most attractive from an EPS standpoint.

However, an investor looking to buy a cheaply priced stock might decide that BP is on sale with a low P/E ratio when compared to the other companies. But when you factor in BP's PEG ratio, it's not all that cheap. You'll have to look closer to see the real numbers behind these values and assumptions about the future that give BP the highest PEG ratio.

The best purchase for the long-term investor, in terms of finding relative value, might be shares of ConocoPhillips. Why? ConocoPhillips had the lowest P/E ratio and the second lowest PEG ratio. Shares of ConocoPhillips might be on sale at this moment and could be a good investment for the long term . . . if your universe was limited to these four companies. You'll have to make investment decisions based on the information you have available. The main idea is that you do your homework and make the best decision possible for your portfolio, instead of buying a stock because you heard someone on TV say it was a great investment. Just like in school, those who do their own work usually reap the most benefit!

As you can see, this type of research isn't easy. Nobody said it would be! Too many people simply watch some random TV program on investing. They hear what company a financial commentator recommends; they think, "Oh, that sounds good"; and they buy stock in that company. Unfortunately, there's one gigantic problem with that approach to investing: you think you're lucky because you happened to watch that TV show, but what happens when you're *not* watching that same show a few weeks later and the same person says, "You know what? I think that company's success is over, and we need to take our profits and get out." There's nothing wrong with listening, but you still need to do your own research, and analyzing that company's ratios is critical before you make a decision to invest.

9

Technical Analysis: It's All about Price, Not Value

How to Read Charts and See Patterns

As mentioned earlier, technical analysis is essentially the art and science of using charts that show the past prices of a particular stock or to track the markets. You can find these charts on www.stockcharts.com, Yahoo! Finance, FINVIZ, MSN Money, and many other Web sites. Many investors like the idea of simply looking at the charts, because all they need to do is look for patterns and indicators that may clue them into the market trend. A trend is simply defined as prices moving in one direction, up or down, for a lengthy period of time—maybe weeks or months. As mentioned in chapter 5, uptrends have a series of higher price highs and higher price lows, whereas downtrends have a series of lower price lows and lower price highs. On a standard chart, an uptrend moves from the bottom left of the chart upward to the upper right side of the chart, whereas a downtrend moves from the upper left side down to the lower right side. A sideways trend has roughly the same price highs and lows over time, and moves sideways across the chart. As discussed in chapter 5, there are three basic market conditions: up, down, and sideways. In addition to moving in these directions, individual stocks can also move in other ways, which I'll discuss in this chapter. I'll also explain how you can read stock charts and how you can use that information not only to choose winning investments, but also to figure out if it's an appropriate time to buy a particular stock.

If you're an average investor who wants to spend only an hour or so a week looking at charts, then technical analysis is a good approach for you. As mentioned earlier, I like to use technical analysis in conjunction with quantitative and fundamental analysis. Before I get to that, however, I'll explain why technical analysis is beneficial in the first place.

Why Should You Use Technical Analysis?

Technical analysis is important in helping investors winning investments select for three reasons:

+ **Markets have trends**. It is assumed that once a market trend is established, it will continue in the same direction because of a supply-and-demand imbalance. By imbalance, we mean buyers continuing to buy, which is the force of demand, over sellers, who represent the force of supply. If there are more buyers than sellers, or the buyers are more aggressive than sellers, then price should rise. If there are more sellers, or the sellers are more aggressive than the buyers, then price should fall. We can look back in time to see the direction of the price movement and then assume that direction could continue, at least for a time. If we're looking at two fundamentally similar stocks, we would prefer to invest in the one that is in an uptrend rather than one in a downtrend. When you have to select between two equally appealing stocks that have similar earnings, ratios, and so on, looking at a chart and finding one stock in an uptrend and the other in a downtrend can break the tie.

+ **Markets are efficient**. What does *market efficiency* mean? It's the theory that everything that can be known about a particular company is already factored into the price of its stock. Markets look forward and "price in" or "discount" (take into account) all available fundamental information about earnings, growth, competition, debt, and other economic factors very, very quickly. There's a saying that "price represents all that can be known and even information that cannot be known by the general public." If we can assume that the current price of a stock is efficient or reflects all available data—we can trust the current price as fair. Inefficiencies don't last long when they exist, and price will return to fair value quickly as new information enters the system. There have been many times we've seen a stock price rise or fall unexpectedly, and then a few days later, we find out what happened through the news. Remember that it takes time for news to reach the public, and people who hear the news first will act on it and that will be reflected immediately in the stock's price. Sometimes you'll see a stock price fall or stay stable on what seems to be really good news because by the time the news became public, the "insiders" had already bid the stock higher to reflect that news.

+ **History repeats itself**. I'm sure you've heard Winston Churchill's saying "Those that fail to study history are doomed to repeat it." Well, that's also true in the market! Certain cycles and long-term price patterns tend to repeat. People who study charts have classified these patterns and given them names like a head and shoulders, flag, saucer, and triangle. Patterns reflect human behavior as they react to information in the market—and let's not forget people tend to be emotional when it comes to money. Think of your own experience—you probably react the same way to the same situations each time they happen in your own life. People tend to react similarly when trading and investing in the market. That's part of what causes price to rise quickly and fall quickly, and the charts leave little footprints of this behavior. These actions and reactions translate into buy-and-sell events, or signals, that show up on price charts. People who study charts try to locate these price patterns and find out what is likely to happen next, based on what has happened in the past. At the very least, they hope to find an early signal as to whether to enter or exit a position.

The Different Types of Stock Charts

As mentioned, the key to technical analysis is analyzing many types of charts. There a number of different stock charts you might see.

+ **Line charts**, the simplest type of charts, are made up of dots that represent a stock's closing price each day, all connected by a line—hence the name *line chart*. These very basic charts don't necessarily show how the price of a stock moved within one day, but rather how it moved over a period of time, such as weeks, months, or years.
+ **Bar charts**, a slightly more complex stock chart, use bars instead of dots. Each day is represented by a vertical line, or bar. The stock's high value for the day marks the top of the bar, and its low value marks the bottom. Often a small horizontal line appears on the left and/or right side of each bar,

which marks the opening and closing price of the stock. Bar charts often include color: green bars indicate that the price ultimately rose during the day, and red indicates it fell.

+ **Candlestick charts** are even more complex than bar charts, but like the bar charts, they show the high and low value for a particular stock in a particular day over a period of time. This chart gets its name from the fact that each day's trading looks like a candle with a wick coming out of each end. As with the bar chart, each day's measurement, or candle, can be shown in green or red, depending on whether the stock's overall value rose or fell.

How to Read a Stock Chart

In order to read and interpret stock charts, you have to understand how charts are constructed and what each piece of information represents. One way technical analysts use charts is to track a stock's price over a specific time. A chart has two basic components: the price and the time period. On one axis, you track data points that represent the price (shown along the vertical axis), and on the other axis, you track a particular period of time (shown along the horizontal axis).

Let's look at a typical bar chart (Figure 5), which measures the price of a sample company's stock over a year. As mentioned, for each date, you will find a corresponding data point. The top of the bar is the high price for the day, the bottom is the low value, and the closing price is marked by the small horizontal line.

On the chart, the vertical axis on the left shows the stock price increasing in $2 increments, from $72 to $94. The horizontal axis at the top shows the time frame during which these prices were tracked: for a period of a year beginning on November 21, 2009, and ending on November 20, 2010. Although this chart

Figure 5. Stock Sideways Trend

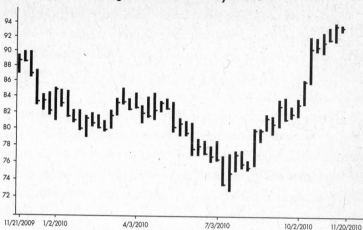

covers one year, you can track prices for a particular month, week, day, or whatever time frame interests you. Regardless of the time period, however, you need to include a data point—in this case a bar—for each trading period during that time. In Figure 5, the trading periods are each week over the year depicted.

When looking at the chart in Figure 5, we can see the current trend of the stock—up, down, or sideways. Because the stock price on this chart has roughly the same price highs and lows over the entire period, it is in a sideways trend. You can see it basically moves sideways across the chart, not in a discernable up or down direction. I'll discuss tips for investing in a sideways trend in a bit. In addition to looking at the trend, we're also watching for any major support or resistance levels that have formed. As mentioned, a support level is the price at which the stock has a limited ability to go lower, and a resistance level is the price at which the stock has a limited ability to go any higher. Those levels may be important reference points into the future, because investors might decide to sell a stock when it rises to a prior resistance level, or buy shares when the stock falls to a prior support level. In Figure 5, the stock price never went under $72 per share, so $72 is an important support level. It could be an ideal price for buying the stock as it's not likely to be available to purchase for less money. Conversely, $94 is the resistance level; you would not want to buy this company's stock at that price because it's likely the most expensive it'll ever be, at least in the near term.

Remember, when looking at charts, you're studying a historical view of the stock. You're seeing what has already happened, but there's no guarantee this trend will continue in the same pattern.

Now that we've covered the basics, let's look at some of the variations on these movements and how you can use this information to make winning investing decisions.

How to Invest When You Find an Upward Trending Pattern

In an *upward trend*, the price of the investment you're tracking is moving higher; it's increasing.

As you will notice in Figure 6, for the most part each successive high price became even higher than the last, and each successive low price became higher than the last low price. An upward trend is a bullish indicator that signals a buying opportunity, because the investment you're tracking may be breaking out through its resistance levels, and beyond.

When you see an uptrend in price, don't get fancy when trying to decide exactly when to buy shares. An uptrend is like a green light that says, "Go ahead and buy." (Assuming you have done all your research.) If the uptrend continues, then over time you could see a rise in your investment, but you might miss out on it if you wait around for a perfect buying opportunity. Keep it simple. If you see an uptrend and your stock has met your criteria for a fundamentally strong company, go ahead and add an initial

Figure 6. Stock Uptrend

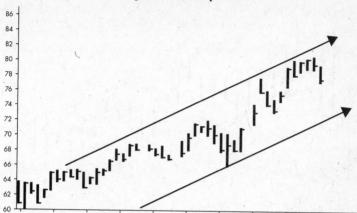

position to your portfolio. If you don't, the stock might just keep rising without you!

How to Invest When You Find a Downtrend

A *downward trend* is the exact opposite of an upward trend, and as its name implies, it indicates that the price of the investment you're tracking is trending down, or decreasing. Each successive high price is lower than the last, and each successive low price is also lower, as shown in Figure 7.

When you see a downward price trend, you definitely won't want to buy that particular stock. A downtrend is like a red light, just like an uptrend is a green light and a sideways trend is a yellow caution light. If you already own the stock, consider selling all or at least part of that investment in order to mitigate your losses. If the downtrend continues, then the price will keep going lower and lower, so if you keep holding the stock in your portfolio, it will be worth less and less. The falling price may signal negative sentiment among investors regarding the investment's

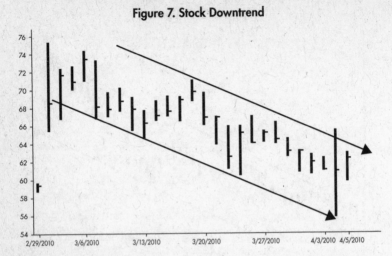

Figure 7. Stock Downtrend

underlying fundamentals, or perhaps there is news that does not favor the outlook. It may be time to take any profits and then start looking to replace the stock with another fundamentally sound company that is in an uptrend.

Selling when the price is dropping is one of the most difficult decisions an investor has to make. That's why I advocate not falling in love with your investments, and instead taking the emotion out of your investing process! In the end, even though it's painful to lose money, it's better to lose $1,000 than almost $5,000 or more, right? As I've said throughout this book, you need to have a long enough time frame in which you can weather the ups and downs of the market, or else you need to watch the market closely so that as soon as you perceive a downward trend, you can sell at least some of your holdings so you don't lose everything.

How to Invest When You Spot a Cyclical Trend

Unfortunately, individual stocks often move in more complex patterns than simply up or down. Stock prices typically fluctuate

Figure 8. Cyclical Trend

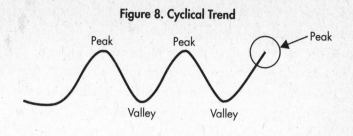

in peaks (high prices) and valleys (low prices), as in the pattern shown in Figure 8. This type of pattern can occur over any time period. Figure 8 shows what a cyclical trend generally looks like so you can easily spot it when looking at an actual stock chart. Obviously, this illustration does not show any particular time period, so this stock's price could be fluctuating back and forth over several days, weeks, or months.

Technical analysts call a cyclical pattern like this a rectangle pattern. If you drew a horizontal line above the price highs and below the price lows and connected the peaks, it would look like a rectangle. A cyclical pattern provides a clear indicator of when it's a good time to sell shares and when it may be a good time to buy shares. The old and simple adage still works: it's best to buy low and sell high. What a cyclical pattern tells you is that when the price hits its historical peak (as shown in Figure 8), it may be a good time to sell your stock, because the price may hit resistance (have a limited ability to go any higher). Of course, it may hit resistance and the price might still soar higher, so if you sell all your shares, you won't realize that future benefit. On the other hand, you will have realized a gain if the peak price is significantly higher than the price you paid for your shares. If the pattern continues and the price does go down, you will be selling your shares at the best price. Then you can get ready to buy shares back again as they fall back to the lower support price—the price at which the stock has a limited ability to go down any further.

When the stock price hits one of its valleys (support), it may be a good time to buy shares, since the trend seems to be (but it is not guaranteed) that the stock price will eventually move back up. Technical analysis can be as simple as that, because again you're making your investing decisions based solely on the price of your investment (in this case, a particular stock). Some investors refer to this strategy as "channel surfing"; the rectangle pattern acts like a sideways trend channel, where investors buy at the bottom of the channel and then sell at the top. There are even Web sites dedicated to this simple strategy. Keep in mind that it does not use any sort of fundamental analysis, but rather uses a historical chart pattern to form assumptions about the future based on what has happened in the past. Though pattern trading like this is used more by traders, who often have shorter time frames for their positions than traditional investors have, investors can still borrow some of their logic and wait until a stock comes into a known support level to buy it.

Let's say you've done your homework, and through quantitative and fundamental analysis you have identified a stock you want to buy, but you just aren't sure when to do so. If you see a rectangle pattern forming, you should buy the stock when it is at the bottom of the rectangle and then hold on to it from there. If you do this, you'll be buying shares at a more favorable price than if you rushed out and bought the stock on the same day you realized the stock is a good buy. It's not something you have to do, but it's what some investors prefer to do.

How to Invest When You See a Pattern of Consolidation

Consolidation is a pattern like that shown in Figure 9. As you can see, this pattern forms a rectangle (shown by lines *A* and *B* in the

Figure 9. Consolidation

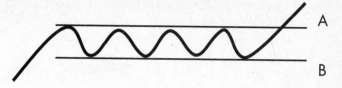

A

B

diagram), and it occurs when pressure is building up in an invest-ment. A consolidation phase is usually a temporary stall in a pat-tern. Investors commonly believe that if an investment has been in an uptrend, or the price has been increasing, and then it begins to consolidate, or stabilize at a particular price or limited price range, then the prevailing uptrend could continue, and a breakout through the resistance level may soon follow.

For example, suppose you're tracking the price of Pfizer (PFE), and it's been fluctuating between $16 and $17 per share. Those fluctuations show that the price is consolidating, so you might expect that if the price breaks through the $17 resistance level it will continue to increase to a higher price. If you believe this will happen, then the time to buy Pfizer is when it first breaks above the top of the consolidated pattern. On the other hand, keep in mind that the consolidation phase can go the other way too. That is, the price of the investment you're tracking might also break through the support level (which is the bottom line, B, in Figure 9), then the price trend may be down from there. Let's say you're watching a stock in a clear rectangle pattern, and you want to add it to your portfolio because it has met your criteria and is showing good fundamentals. You can either buy the stock as its price trades at the established lower support area (which gives you a better entry), or wait until the price rises and closes above the up-per resistance line. You can set alerts in Yahoo! Finance and other Web sites to notify you via email or text message when a stock has risen above a certain price. You would look at the chart, then buy the stock if you are convinced the price has risen above resistance and is likely to continue its uptrend.

How to Invest When You See a "Congestion" Pattern

Sometimes there's no pattern at all to the price of the investment you're tracking. For example, your price chart might look something like the one shown in Figure 10. This pattern (or actually,

Figure 10. Congestion

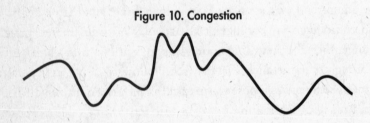

lack of a pattern) usually indicates that investors are confused about the direction for that investment. This is why the price is moving all over the place. The best way to invest when you see congestion is not to invest; it's better to wait until a clearer picture emerges and you can see how the price is trending. Remember that charts are the final step in your process before buying an investment. If the chart is not giving you a clear signal, it might be best to stand aside until you do see a clear uptrend or pattern, or to consider investing in another stock that is showing a better uptrend or clearer pattern of support and resistance.

Monitoring the Ten-Month Moving Average

So far we've been talking about monitoring individual investments, but you can also use charts to track the overall market. One way to do this is by monitoring the *ten-month moving average*. In chapter 5 we talked about the two hundred-day and fifty-week moving averages. Well, the ten-month moving average takes the closing price at the end of the month for each of the last ten months, and then it takes the average of those ten prices. It gives the average price of the stock for a period of about a year. The value on your stock chart reflects that value, plotted as a line. Remember, as a new month ends, the last data point—the price eleven months ago—is eliminated. Then the current close—last month—is added, so the line is the moving average of monthly closes.

For example, if you look at the S&P 500 and the monthly returns over time, you can follow where the stock market is trending. If the average price of the last ten-months is rising, then you can be somewhat assured that the market is in an uptrend. But if the average price of the last ten-months is falling, and you can see that in the direction or slope of the moving average, then the trend of the market or stock is falling. (You can find ten-month moving averages on www.stockcharts.com and other money sites.

Figure 11. Moving Average Graph

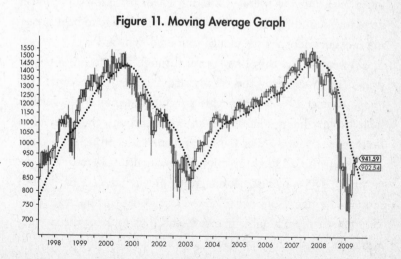

To track the S&P 500, you could type in $SPX where the page says "choose a type of chart" and "enter a symbol.")

So far in this chapter we've been looking at bar charts. For the next example, we'll use a candlestick chart.

When looking at charts, you'll be able to select the particular parameters you want to look at. For example, you can choose a time frame such as daily or weekly.

In the candlestick chart in Figure 11, you can see the closing price from month to month, and a thin line going through them: that line is the ten-month moving average. It's important to look at the slope of the moving average. Notice how the average itself flattens and then turns down in late 2000 to indicate a change to a downtrend. Then also notice the same flattening arc that gives way to a new uptrend in mid-2003, and the same flattening and curving over to a new downtrend in early 2008. When defining a trend, an uptrend is a series of higher high prices and higher low prices, with price being above the ten-month moving average, and the ten-month moving average rising in value or slope, month after month. For a downtrend, look for price to be underneath the ten-month moving average, making lower price lows and lower price highs, and for the ten-month moving average to be decreasing in value month-after-month (sloped downward).

Wherever the thin line breaks through the closing monthly prices (represented by the candlesticks), it's an early signal of a changing trend. Of course, this is hindsight, but it gives you a look at what happened. Price can break through the ten-month average for a few months, but always look to see if the price keeps moving in the original direction. Don't make any trading or investment decisions just because price breaks under a ten-month moving average. Look for price to close under that average for at least two or more months in a row, and then look for the moving average to begin to curve down.

For example, in the chart in Figure 11, consider the time frame between 1998 and 2003, which looks like a big mountain. Notice two things: first, generally speaking, the candlesticks (i.e., the monthly price ranges of the S&P index) are above the thin line: that's the ten-month moving average. Each candlestick represents the actual monthly range in price for the S&P 500 index. What you see here is that the simple moving average, on the day this chart was created, was 902.54.

The moving average is simply a calculation of the closing prices for the previous ten months; if you take each month's closing price and average them over the last ten months, that's the average. Then every single month, you calculate the moving average for the previous ten months, and you place a point on the chart. The points are then connected with a line.

When you look at the trend in Figure 11 over time—look at 1998 through the first half of 2000—you can see that the closing prices (of SPX, the S&P 500 large-cap index) are for the most part *above* the ten-month moving average. Then, in about the second half of 2000, closing prices moved *below* the average, and they stayed consistently below there for some time. In 2003 the trend reversed, and then the S&P 500 index price stayed mostly above the average until the second half of 2007. Then they went below the moving average again—dramatically. From there, they stayed below for most of the next two years. What you, as an investor, should note from this type of chart is very simple: when the prices you're tracking are above a rising moving average, the market trend is said to be moving higher; when the prices you're tracking are below a declining moving average, the market trend is down. While that's a very simple way to read the chart, it's all most investors need to know. There's no need to make it complicated.

> ### ▓▓▓ Quick and Dirty Tip
>
> If the current market is above a ten-month moving average that is rising, then it is considered an up market, which makes it an uptrend.

However, there's still one problem with an uptrend that may change. Look again at the chart in Figure 11, specifically at the last point on the right-hand side, where the thin line is captured at 902.54 and the candlestick prices are captured at 941.59. Notice that in the uptrend, the thin line is going up—that is, it's moving further away from and higher than the candlestick prices below it. Similarly, the moving average is going down: the two lines are moving farther away from each other. Is there the possibility that you have a continual downtrend, and you'll still be over the thin line? Again, if you look at the far right-hand side, which shows the data for the date on which the example chart was created, you'll notice it looks like it's beginning to move in an uptrend, because the closing prices have just crossed above the moving average line. However, the thin line is still declining.

One of two things has to occur. Either the upturn is not yet confirmed, and it's not going to continue in that direction, or the moving line is going to turn upward eventually, and we'll get a double confirmation that not only are we above the uptrend, but the moving average line turns positive as well.

While we've examined the S&P 500, you can do this exact same work for any stock that you want to add to your portfolio. Remember, we use quantitative analysis in the forms of screening to find stocks that meet our specific criteria. After we have a list of about thirty to fifty stocks or so, we then want to narrow that list down to maybe ten to twenty stocks. We can do this using fundamental analysis, comparing ratios of companies, and looking for companies with superior ratios and prospects for continued growth. Then when we finally decide what stocks we want to add to our portfolio, we should take a close look at the charts described in this chapter, specifically looking at whether each stock is in an uptrend and whether it is above its ten-month moving average. Only then should we buy the stock. Suppose there are three stocks that meet both our screening criteria and our analysis criteria for the fundamental ratios. When we look at the charts of these three stocks, one stock is in a clear rising uptrend, another is in a clear falling downtrend, and another is moving sideways. The chart has made the final decision for us: invest in the stock showing a consistent rising uptrend over time.

The Bottom Line

The charts shown in this chapter include only the most basic patterns. There are lengthy tomes written on the subject of technical analysis, which show every type of pattern you might encounter when tracking the price of an investment. There are hundreds of trend patterns and indicators and a myriad of ways to use technicals. The quick and dirty tip on technical analysis is that it's just another way for you to research possible investments. After you've done your research—which means scanning for stocks that meet your criteria, then looking over the balance sheets and analyst reports, and comparing ratios of companies—technical analysis can give you the final piece of the puzzle you need in order to add a stock to your portfolio. Your goal is to find fundamentally solid companies that have above-average growth forecasts and better ratios than their peers. But you shouldn't rush out to buy a stock just because the fundamentals are strong. You should also look at its chart to make sure the price is in an uptrend and that price is above a ten-month rising moving average. If you have to choose between two stocks that are similar from a fundamental analysis and ratio standpoint, you should always buy the one showing an uptrend on its price charts as opposed to the one showing a downtrend; otherwise, wait to buy the stock when it breaks above a horizontal resistance area during a sideways trend. After all, if you keep track of what the price is doing, it should give you a good indication of what other investors think about the value of that investment.

10

Specialty/Alternative Investments

*Gold and Other Precious Metals, Food and
Other Commodities, Real Estate and REITs
(Real Estate Investment Trusts)*

So far in this book, I've been focusing on general markets. However, in addition to these traditional investments, you can really invest in anything that you think will make you a profit. Some common alternative investments include gold and other precious metals, food and other commodities, energy (such as crude oil or natural gas), real estate or real estate investment trusts, and foreign currencies. I'll discuss how to invest in each of these.

Investing in Gold or Other Metals

Many people who invest in metals invest primarily in gold, although you can also invest in silver, copper, platinum, and palladium. Palladium, a member of the platinum metals group, is steel white in color and doesn't tarnish in the air, as silver will. There are a number of different ways to invest in metals. You may invest directly, by actually purchasing them, or you may invest in a metals ETF or a stock associated with a metal, such as Freeport McMoran (FCX), a company that mines and sell metals used in building and construction. This stock will likely do best when construction and the housing markets are booming.

If your research leads you to believe that the price of industrial metals will be moving higher and will continue to go up, you might consider investing in companies like Joy Global Inc. (JOYG) and Bucyrus (BUCY), which manufacture equipment and machinery used to mine precious and industrial metals. As demand for metals increases, so should the demand for the equipment used to mine them. On the other hand, if there's a drop in the price of industrial metals and commodities, then these companies may have too much equipment to sell, with too few buyers. That's another reason you need to keep current with economic trends and the global economy.

Now let's take a closer look at investing in precious metals rather than industrial metals. Many investors prefer precious metals as an investment primarily because they are tangible. You can actually handle and physically store gold and silver, unlike a share of stock. And unlike a paper investment, nobody can take metals from you. That tangibility provides comfort to many investors, staving off the fear they feel when they invest in intangible, paper assets. As an example, you could wake up one morning to the news that a company in which you are invested has declared bankruptcy, making the value of the shares of stock you own absolutely worthless. But you'll never wake up to the headline that all the gold and silver in the world are suddenly worthless.

Also, many precious metals investors have a special interest in gold because they believe it will increase in value forever. Gold has its place because it has acted as an inflationary protection mechanism, and it's a tangible item that has intrinsic value, as op-posed to the U.S. dollar or any other paper currency. Remember that economists often expect a normal annual rate of inflation of 2 percent to 3 percent per year, but when inflation is higher than 5 percent, the value of the dollars you hold are becoming worth less in real terms year after year. However, if you invest in gold instead of stocks, bonds, or even cash in times of high inflation, you may see that gold rises along with, or higher than, the infla-tion rate. As such, it is beneficial in inflationary periods to own gold instead of assets like currencies that are declining due to the rate of inflation.

Personally, I believe you have room in your portfolio for both paper investments and gold or other precious metals, depending on when you buy, of course. As with all investments, you should obvi-ously try your best to buy low and sell high. When you see the outlook for massive inflation, that's usually a good time to purchase gold. You can track inflation trends by watching energy prices, spe-cifically crude oil, along with government reports on the producer price index and the consumer price index. Anything above a 2 per-cent to 3 percent annual increase in the rate of inflation is consid-ered high, while anything above 6 percent is exceptionally high.

You can buy gold in several different ways. For one, you can buy the actual commodity, either in gold bars or jewelry. But un-less you have your own personal vault, you'll need to store your gold in a safety deposit box at your local bank or other secure lo-cation. Another way to buy gold is through ETFs. Many people buy gold through ETFs because they don't want gold bars or bul-lion lying around their house. Think about what would happen if you had gold in your house and had to evacuate because of fire or flood? Not fun. My company buys gold for client portfolios via gold ETFs because they rather accurately track the value of gold.

When Should You Consider Investing in Gold?

Many people consider investing in gold, other precious metals, and other specialty investments particularly during inflationary times and times of fear. In general, investing in gold and other precious metals helps to diversify your portfolio, and so I suggest you consider investing up to about 5 percent of your total portfolio in these assets. I don't recommend much more than 5 percent though, because our research has shown that, in general, gold and the like will not keep pace with the returns you may receive on investments in equity markets.

Quick and Dirty Tip

You could buy a car today with the value of gold you have. And in ten years or even fifty years, you should be able to buy a car with *that same amount of gold.* In contrast, in fifty years you might need one hundred times as much paper currency to buy that same car, because of inflation. That's why gold is a good hedge against inflation: it is expected to retain its value, regardless of inflation.

Investing in Commodities

Another alternate investment option to include in your portfolio is *commodities*, basic goods that are uniform among producers. For example, corn is a commodity because an ear of corn grown on one farm is pretty much the same as an ear of corn grown on another farm (although the farmers themselves may argue about that!). In contrast, products that are designed—like furniture or jewelry—are not commodities because one designer's ring will be markedly different from another's. Many other foods besides corn are commodities, such as wheat, sugar, and soybeans. Other examples of commodities include oil (as in petroleum) and natural gas. You can invest in many commodities through a commodity exchange. Such an exchange is similar to a stock exchange except that the traders are buying and selling commodities instead of stocks. One such place is the Chicago Mercantile Exchange (CME). The problem with investing in commodities directly on an exchange is twofold: first, you may have to invest a significant amount of money, and second, even if you invest only $1,000, you may at some point have to take possession of the commodity you've purchased. This means that someday a person driving a truckload of coffee beans or pork bellies may drive up your street and want to unload on your front lawn.

Fortunately, you can also buy commodities through ETFs, which is what my company does for our clients, so that we don't have to worry about the possibility of taking physical possession of the actual commodity. For example, in the past we've invested in the following funds (among others):

- **DBA** (PowerShares DB Agriculture Fund), whose holdings include soybean, corn, sugar, and wheat futures
- **DBC** (PowerShares DB Commodity Index), whose top holdings include heating oil and crude oil futures, gold, and corn and wheat futures
- **DBO** (PowerShares DB Oil Fund), which essentially tracks an index of futures contracts on light sweet crude oil and is intended to reflect the general performance of crude oil

I'm not saying *you* should invest in these funds; these are only examples of what we've invested in from time to time. Rather than investing in only stocks or bonds, we like investing in commodities because they complement and diversify a portfolio.

As you can see, some of the ETFs just mentioned hold agricultural commodities only, some metals only, some oil, and some a mix. Again, investing in commodities is a great way to invest some of the money in your portfolio because it gives you the truest diversification against paper assets, which are obviously much different than commodities. We like investing in food commodities because all research continues to show that the population of the world is growing dramatically. This type of investment seems like a great opportunity over the long term, because there will be an ongoing need to feed everyone. In contrast, you can't really use gold as an easy form of currency unless economic conditions get very, very bad.

There's a tremendous amount of information on investing in commodities that is beyond the scope of this book. This section was intended simply to introduce the why and how of diversifying into commodity alternatives. If you're interested in investing in commodities, you should start paying attention to global trends—not only economic trends, but also, for example, weather patterns that affect agricultural commodities, or how sugar is being used as an energy alternative to ethanol.

Investing in Real Estate and REITs (Real Estate Investment Trusts)

Real estate is another investment you might want to consider. There are entire books written about buying and managing properties, but that's not what this section is going to focus on. I don't believe that's manageable for the average investor. Personally, I'm not a big real estate fan, and I never have been, even though real estate is often the largest investment that most people own. But that real estate investment is usually a person's own home, and you should not view your home as an investment. Instead, you should look at it as the place where you live, and you should enjoy it as such. If that property happens to appreciate in value over time, great; but don't count on making a killing on the sale of your home, because you have no idea what the housing market (or the economy in general) will look like when you're ready to sell. Investing in real estate can be another excellent way to diversify your portfolio, and if you're interested in doing so, I suggest you consider investing in real estate investment trusts, or REITS. Pronounced "reets," REITs are pooled assets, much like a mutual fund. But instead of pooling shares in stocks from a variety of companies, REITs pool investments in apartments or commercial buildings, including office buildings, nursing homes, hospitals, shopping malls, and other diversified properties. REITs, which are actively traded on a stock exchange like the NYSE, often provide the potential for good income because traditionally they pay dividends. These dividends are usually above market rate, since rents are coming in regularly, usually from long-term leases on the underlying properties.

There are all kinds of REITS to choose from. There are specialized REITs, such as health-care REITs that comprise properties that biotech and health-care companies rent. Many investors believe that health-care REITS are a safe bet because research shows that the businesses they invest in have good cash flows. These biotech and health-care industries are growing, and so it's more likely that the businesses within those industries will stay in business—and therefore those tenants will be paying rent on a regular basis, which means cash is coming in. There are also REITs that invest in apartment complexes only; some that are retail-oriented only; and some that hold restaurant properties only. Investors like REITs because they usually provide income through pay dividends, and they help diversify a portfolio.

When considering investing in a REIT, one area to look at is the occupancy rate of the properties comprising the REIT. Are they 90 percent occupied? Or are they only 50 percent occupied? Obviously, the higher the occupancy rate, the safer your investment will be. Also, you should know what the terms of the lease are. In general, look for leases that are very long term, so you can ensure that the properties will continue to generate cash flow.

Keep in mind that because REITs are *real estate* trusts, they are susceptible to the ups and downs of the real estate market. So, for example, during the downturn that began in 2007, it wasn't only residential real estate that was affected very badly, but commercial real estate as well. Here's an example: General Growth Properties, a REIT that owned and operated malls, went bankrupt in 2009. It was the biggest bankruptcy of a REIT ever. There are default risks associated with REITs too (*all* investments have risks), but many of the assets inside the REIT are illiquid (in other words, you can't sell them immediately for cash). Moreover, many REITs are very difficult to value because the value of the underlying real estate is a moving target. Because it is less liquid, it's not as easy to sell as a stock, for example, or a mutual fund, where you often know the exact value of the underlying investments. As with all other investments, look at the financials underlying the REIT, as well as the quality of its management. Finally, there are many other different ways to invest in real estate through REITS, but again, that's beyond the scope of this book.

The analysis of a REIT is much different than the analysis of a stock, because instead of looking at P/E ratios or earnings (as described in chapter 8), you look at what's called *FFO*, or *Funds From Operations*. It's on par with earnings, but it's different.

You can also buy real estate through ETFs. That is by far the easiest way to invest in real estate—that is, in an ETF that tracks a particular real estate benchmark. The iShares real estate fund (IYR) is probably the most popular real estate investment among investors who want quick exposure to the real estate market. There are dozens of ETFs you could invest in, including inverse (short) real estate funds to use as a hedge or a speculative investment if you feel real estate values may be headed down in the future. Search Google, Yahoo! Finance, or MSN Money for lists of REITs and real estate–based ETFs. It's best to avoid illiquid ETFs that trade less than fifty thousand shares per day; the more shares traded per day, the better.

Real estate traditionally has been a diversifier—at least it was prior to the 2007 fallout—and it probably will be again, in time. If you're interested in investing in real estate, pay close attention to the construction and housing trends. Obviously when building is increasing, real estate is a good investment, but when construction is falling, you may want to shy away from real estate altogether.

Investing in real estate has often been thought of as a long-term hold rather than a short-term traded investment. It's usually best as a diversifier rather than a stand-alone investment.

Quick and Dirty Tip

The easiest way to invest in real estate is through a pooled asset, such as a mutual fund, a REIT, or an ETF. With this type of investment, you should let the people who are managing it (who are experts in their area) have the reins, because real estate is valued much differently than most other investments.

Finally, most investors should allocate a maximum of 10 percent of their total portfolio to real estate. Again, that's excluding their home, which shouldn't be considered part of their investing portfolio.

Investing in Energy

Once considered a boring industry sector, energy has become a rather fascinating obsession for many investors. Let's begin the discussion of energy by separating it into its two primary components: renewable energy (like solar and wind power) and nonrenewable energy (fossil fuels like coal and oil).

As we know, there is a finite amount of oil under the ground. That's why oil is a nonrenewable energy source—once it's used up, it's gone. For this reason, many people are very concerned about it, because it is believed that we won't have enough oil in the future, and that's a scary proposition. This panic was one of the catalysts for the surge in oil prices during the summer of 2008; the other was rampant speculation by energy traders.

There is a frantic race on to find the next energy source, or to become much more efficient with the use of our current energy sources, especially for transportation. Heating is different. Energy consumption is an interesting phenomenon because, as with food, there is a continual requirement, and it's not replaceable. If we don't have oil or other kinds of fuel to meet our transportation needs, the world economy will crack, because everything in an economy is based on something moving somebody—or something getting somewhere. In order to run and expand an economy, energy is required. It is used in virtually every aspect of manufacturing, in sales and retail, and in other consumer-based businesses. Think about it: without fuel, the economy will just grind to a halt, frozen in position. That's why there is such a focus on oil and alternative energy sources.

Therefore energy may be a great area to invest in over time. However, energy has a lot more potential emotion and controversy involved in it because it deals with *future expectations of finite issues.* Energy is somewhat like real estate on a beach: there's only so much waterfront, so there are only so many properties that can be built there.

When you "trade" or invest in energy, you can do it in several ways. You can buy the actual energy source itself, but you may have to buy a tanker filled with oil! You might be able to store bars of gold in a safety deposit box, but they generally won't let you store crude oil in them! Only the biggest banks and investment firms, such as Goldman Sachs (GS) and J.P. Morgan (JPM), are able to purchase energy sources. If you don't trade futures contracts, a type of investing too complex for this book, then the other way is to invest directly in companies like Exxon Mobil, Chevron, or in a major ETF, which allows for instant exposure and diversification. You can also invest in companies that specialize in other energy sources, such as coal and natural gas, and those that are mining it up from the ground. Or you can invest in companies involved in the processing of the energy to make it usable, such as Occidental Petroleum Corporation (OXY).

When you research the many different types of energy companies, if you're an average investor, you're probably going to lean toward investing in stocks or ETFs. Two of the most popular energy-based ETFs are the United States Oil Fund (USO) and the United States Natural Gas Fund (UNG). There is also the Energy Sector Fund (XLE), which is very popular among investors. Learn about the energy-based ETF you are considering, and then buy shares in that fund as you would a stock. You can also buy stock in a company that has energy as the main component of what it does.

Investing in energy is a great diversifier for your portfolio. Energy also gives you diversification into a hard asset, something that for the most part is more tangible. For instance, if more goods are being manufactured and transported, there may be more natural gas usage in factories that use natural gas in the manufacturing process.

Like food and water, we all have to use energy, either through transportation or to heat our homes. As an investor, you have opportunities to invest either in companies that produce or refine energy sources for use by consumers, or in the physical commodity of crude oil or natural gas itself. It's harder to store barrels of crude oil than it is bullions of gold, so most investors will instead purchase an exchange-traded fund like USO or UNG, which are similar to the gold (GLD) ETF, to gain investment exposure to oil and natural gas. Alternatively, investors can buy ETFs like XLE that represent a basket of energy companies so they are more diversified than if they bought one or two individual companies in the energy sector of the economy.

Investing in Currencies

If you want to add another diversifying technique to your portfolio, consider investing in, or trading, currencies via the foreign exchange market, also called the Forex market or FX market. A currency transaction is simply investing in one currency, like the U.S. dollar, against another, like the British pound. Investing in currencies is a relational investment: you're buying or selling one currency against another. The Forex refers to "foreign exchange, or currencies," and it is the method by which currencies are converted across the globe. This market helps set the exchange rates you'll pay when you exchange your dollars for euros when you visit Europe or for yen when you travel to Japan. It might be easier to visit other countries if there were a single global currency, but that's not the way the world works; each country has its own currency. As such, the Forex market exists to facilitate simple currency conversions between foreign governments, banks, and individuals.

The Forex Market

The Forex market is mainly an electronic exchange of currencies. It does not have a central location like the N.Y. Stock Exchange, which has its headquarters on Wall Street in Manhattan. The purpose of the foreign exchange market is to help facilitate international trade and investment. There are financial centers around the world including Tokyo, London, and New York, but none of them claim to be the "global capital" of the foreign exchange markets. But London has the largest daily volume, at roughly $1.3 trillion, which is just over 35 percent of the total global volume, so today it's considered the largest hub for foreign exchange. The Forex market helps businesses convert one currency to another. For example, it permits a U.S. business to import European goods and pay in euros, even though the business's income is in U.S. dollars. Also, McDonald's (MCD) restaurants that operate in Europe take in euros, and these euros must be converted into U.S. dollars for McDonald's to use as revenues from its overseas operations. Any U.S. company that does business overseas will eventually convert currencies back and forth through the Forex market.

How to Invest in Foreign Currencies

If you're interested in investing in foreign currencies, I suggest avoiding the Forex market and investing instead in currency ETFs. I provide a list of popular currency ETFs on the next page.

If you think the U.S. dollar is going to be stronger against foreign currencies over the next few months or years, consider adding a U.S. dollar ETF to your growing portfolio. The most popular dollar ETF is known by the symbol (UUP). It will rise when the U.S. dollar rises against foreign currencies. The mix in the UUP fund is a basket of foreign currencies similar to the U.S. Dollar Index.

But what if you want to diversify by investing in foreign currencies that you think will rise relative to other currencies? That's when you need to learn all about foreign-currency ETFs. The most liquid and common currency ETFs are known as "CurrencyShares" trusts. The first two letters of these ETFs is often "FX." It makes sense if you think about it—the FX is a shortened way to say Forex.

After the U.S. dollar, the second most common currency ETF is the euro, which trades under the symbol FXE. To see how the euro is performing relative to a basket of other foreign currencies, including the U.S. Dollar Index, you would type symbol FXE into your favorite financial Web site. Then you'll be able to see information and prices on the CurrencyShares Euro Trust. As always, be sure to read the prospectus and all the information you can find on an ETF, including what the expense ratios and fees are, before investing.

Some of the foreign-currency ETFs you can invest in include:

+ British Pound (FXB)
+ Japanese Yen (FXY)
+ Canadian Dollar (FXC)
+ Swedish Krona (FXS)
+ Swiss Franc (FXF)
+ Mexican Peso (FXM)

Why Add Foreign Currencies to Your Portfolio?

Why would you add foreign currencies to your portfolio? The purpose of these currency ETFs is to open up a whole new world of investing, allowing you to diversify your investments away from the U.S. dollar.

Investors invest in these funds to gain exposure to other currencies and ensure that they can maintain purchasing power should the dollar decline in value. The U.S. dollar does not always have to rise; sometimes the value of the dollar falls relative to other currencies. Always think of currencies as relative strength relationships, where one is rising while another currency is falling in value. When you think of currencies, think of exchange rates.

Let's use a real-world example about currency pairs. Let's say you are an American citizen who visited Germany, France, and Spain in 2002. When you landed at the airport, you converted your dollars into euros either at a bank or a foreign currency–exchange office. In 2002, the exchange rate was 1 to 1, so for every U.S. dollar you exchanged, you got back 1 euro. So $100 equaled 100 euros. When a currency is equal to another currency, we say that they are at parity.

Now let's say you decided to visit Europe again in 2008. This time when you arrived at the airport, the exchange rate was 1.5 to 1. It took $1.50 to convert into 1 euro. This time it took $150 to get the same 100 euros you bought in 2002. It was 50 percent more expensive to convert dollars into euros in 2008 than it was in 2002! In real-world terms, if you bought a meal that cost 10 euros in 2002, it cost you $10. However, that same 10-euro meal in 2008 actually cost you $15 because you had to convert your dollars to euros. A European traveler in 2008 who visited the United States got the benefit of the stronger euro to the weaker dollar. If he bought a $10 meal, it was the equvalent of about 6.67 euros. The meal cost the same in both countries—10 units of the currency—but the meal cost less for the European traveler in the United States than for the American traveler in Europe. Keep in mind that in 2002, the meals would have cost exactly the same on both sides of the Atlantic. That's a real-world example of how currencies change. A steady change in the value of your currency mainly affects you if you travel overseas to a country whose currency is stronger than your own.

As an investor, you can hedge against major trends in currencies, such as a decline in the value of the dollar relative to other currencies. By buying the respective currency ETF, you will gain a profit in your investment if the value of the currency continues to increase. However, if you believe a currency will increase in the future against the dollar, you might exchange your dollars for units of a foreign currency, such as the euro or Japanese yen, through a currency exchange at your local bank. Because this encounters the problem of storage, like holding on to bars of gold or barrels of crude oil, most investors choose to gain exposure to a rising foreign currency, or hedge against a falling dollar, by purchasing respective currency exchange-traded funds (ETFs).

If you want to trade currencies, it's a good idea to start by looking at a country's economic outlook. Examine such factors as the country's GDP and its exports, and find out what's going on in that country politically, economically, financially, socially, and so on. If that country is relatively economically weak compared to another, its currency will probably be weak too. Thus the country's currency might be going down in value, as opposed to the currency of a more stable and growing country. So you wouldn't want to invest in a declining currency, unless you're shorting it, of course.

How do you figure out what to buy? The easiest way is to look at which countries are stronger than others, so you can do a comparative analysis. If a country's economy looks like it's going to be very strong due to a surge in its output, then consider investing in its currency over some other country's currency. Remember, currencies are quoted as relative strength pairs, with the currency of the economy that is growing faster rising in price, relative to the currency of the economy that is either contracting or growing slower, which will decline. Think relative strength when it comes to currencies. Buy shares in the currency ETF of the country that you believe has a stronger economy and will be benefiting by a rise in its respective currency. Keep in mind you're not investing in country ETFs, but rather in the currency of the country.

Sometimes the economy of a country can grow while its currency does not, so remember that currency and economy are not always linked. There's no minimum investment via ETFs; you can buy as little as a single share, which might be only $50 or $25. However, it's definitely more expensive to invest via the traditional Forex markets.

Finally, investing in currencies the way I'm describing here is usually a longer-term trade. You could do it as a day trader, buying and selling within a single day, but you probably wouldn't do that. Instead, you would look at what direction the country in which you're interested is moving. For example, is the country getting into trouble because of political instability, wars, or other reasons? When a tidal wave hit Phuket, Thailand, in 2004, it was fairly obvious that it was going to devastate the country, and possibly push down the value of the currency. Thus investors might have wanted to stay away from investing in that region until there was a turnaround. The potential default and bankruptcy of Greece, Spain, and other European countries made the headlines in May 2010 and sent the value of the euro much lower. When there was talk of up to five countries falling deeper into financial crisis, it was a time to avoid the euro.

If you are a more active investor, once or twice a month, you will probably follow the trends of currencies around the world, and add a little piece to your portfolio from time to time, depending on conditions. To maintain a well-diversified portfolio, the maximum you may want to include in terms of currency exposure is about 5 percent to 10 percent of your total portfolio.

The Bottom Line

Now you know a few quick and dirty guidelines to alternative investments. You have some insight into investing in precious metals—especially gold, although there are others—so you can decide if you want to devote part of your portfolio to these. You know more about investing in commodities, my favorite being those in the agriculture and energy sectors, because there's always going to be a need for food products and travel. You know something about how to invest in real estate—but not in terms of your own home, which you should view only as the place in which you live; if it happens to appreciate over time, great, but don't count on it! Instead, I believe the best way to invest in real estate is through real estate investment trusts, or REITs, which are essentially mutual funds of property. Unless you're going to buy and sell real estate as a career or a business, the safest approach to real estate investing is as part of a larger, more diversified portfolio. You also know now how to invest in energy and foreign currency.

If you're feeling a bit overwhelmed by all the investing information presented so far, you may decide that you need a little help. If that's the case, don't worry. Let's turn to chapter 11, which offers some quick and dirty tips on finding the right financial advisor to help you manage and invest your money wisely and, we hope, profitably!

11

Choosing a Financial Advisor

If You Decide You Want More
Guidance (Instead of DIY)

After reading this far, you may have decided that you'd rather not spend a lot of your free time managing your investments. You may prefer to spend your time either working to make more money or relaxing and enjoying the money you've earned already. That's certainly your choice. You also may feel that while you want to be an active investor, you still need a little guidance. It's easy to get overwhelmed by all of the financial information that's available. But you can't let information overload get in your way. Don't let "analysis paralysis" take over and prevent you from reaching your financial goals. If you're feeling overwhelmed, find someone to help. In this chapter I'll tell you how you can find a qualified, experienced financial advisor to help you.

The Different Types of Financial Advisors

The first thing you need to know when hiring a financial advisor is that he or she should have certain qualifications. Your financial advisor should be a Certified Financial Planner (CFP®). This certification is important because it proves that your advisor is committed and hardworking enough to pass the CFP® examination. That's not easy. The CFP® exam is rigorous and exhaustive, so anyone who has received this designation has already proved to be committed to this profession.

Although the CFP® is considered the gold standard of personal financial planners, there are also other designations that you may come across when seeking a qualified advisor. These include:

+ **ChFC® (Chartered Financial Consultant):** Financial advisors with this designation have taken many of same courses as CFP®s, but they haven't taken the comprehensive exam required to receive CFP® certification.
+ **CLU (Chartered Life Underwriter):** CLU® is considered to be the most respected insurance designation. It focuses more on life insurance planning, which includes estate planning and financial planning, but it does not focus specifically on investing.
+ **PFS (Personal Financial Specialist):** PFS is a credential for CPAs (certified public accountants) who specialize in personal financial planning. This credential is given by the AICPA (American Institute of Certified Public Accountants). To qualify as a PFS, the advisor must have at least 3,000 hours of financial planning experience and continuing education within the past five years, and must have passed the comprehensive and rigorous personal financial planning exam.

✦ CFA (Chartered Financial Analyst): CFA is given only to candidates who pass the CFA exams. There are three levels of exams, and each requires 250 hours of study. The CFA is more often a professional financial analyst, rather than a personal financial planner: for example, CFAs often work for investment companies, mutual funds, broker-dealer investment banks, banks, consulting firms, insurance companies, hedge funds, pensions and foundations, and research and academic institutions.

Quick and Dirty Tip

Consider hiring a Certified Financial Planner (CFP®). This qualification requires passing a very difficult test, so anyone who is a CFP should be hardworking, knowledgeable, and committed to a career as a financial advisor.

The Four Different Ways You May Be Charged

Before you hire anyone, be aware that financial advisors make their money in different ways. This is important to know because how they make money sometimes can affect how your investments make money. Here are four ways that financial advisors charge their clients:

1. pay-per-trade
2. fee-only
3. fee-based
4. commission-based

Now let's take a look at each type in more detail.

Pay-per-Trade Financial Advisors

A pay-per-trade financial advisor earns their money by charging you every time he or she trades a stock or any other investment on your behalf. In other words, if the advisor suggests you buy stock in Microsoft (MSFT) and you agree, you will be charged a transaction fee to buy that stock. For the most part, a pay-per-trade advisor is considered a "broker" who merely assists you with your trades, rather than providing investing advice. In other words, when working with this type of advisor, you will likely be the one who decides you want to buy shares of Microsoft, and the advisor will simply handle that transaction.

These days, most people don't really have a broker as they did several decades ago ("Call my broker! Sell everything!"). Instead, this type of pay-per-trade financial advisor is more likely part of a service that many brokerage houses offer. Some financial companies, such as TD Ameritrade, employ advisors who receive a base salary and then earn bonuses based on the thousands of flat-rate trading fees the company earns from its clients.

Fee-Only Financial Advisors

Fee-only financial advisors charge you a standard hourly fee, a flat fee, or a percentage fee for their advice and portfolio management. In addition, they may also charge an annual fee associated with the types of investment management that you and your advisor agree on. It's often a percentage fee based on the assets that your advisor manages for you; you're paying for ongoing advice and support beyond the initial consultation.

Fee-Based Financial Advisors

Fee-based financial advisors charge fees in a variety of ways. They may charge a flat hourly rate when they spend time talking to and working with you, plus a fee for managing your portfolio. They may also receive a commission on investments they purchase on your behalf. Think of this advisor as a blend of the fee-only and commission-based programs.

Commission-Based Financial Advisors

Commission-based financial advisors are similar to any other commission-based salespeople. They are paid only when you implement their suggestions to buy stocks, mutual funds, ETFs, and so on. If you don't take their advice or recommendations, you don't pay them anything and they don't make any money. Therefore, remember that they may not always have *your* best interests in mind.

> **Quick and Dirty Tip**
>
> How your financial advisor makes money often affects how you make money on the investments he or she recommends.

What to Look for When Choosing a Financial Advisor

There are a few guidelines to keep in mind when looking to hire a financial advisor. Here's a quick and dirty overview.

✦ **Your financial advisor should be a full-time financial advisor.** Don't hire someone who offers financial planning services as a sideline to some other type of work. Financial planning is a full-time job for professionals—you're hiring a professional because you don't have the time to devote to investing yourself.

✦ **Your financial advisor should be independent.** Independent advisors can better meet your individual investing needs because they are not associated with a big insurance or brokerage firm. That may sound counterintuitive; you may be thinking, "Why wouldn't I want to hire someone who works for a well-known, reputable company?" The answer is that many advisors who work for a big firm may be required, or incentivized by the company, to sell you—or at least persuade you aggressively to buy—some of the products the company markets. Obviously, you don't want to be pressured into buying anything, especially if that investment is more in your advisor's best interests—via a commission, for example—than in your best interests. In contrast, independent advisors aren't bound by a narrow range of products or services, so they can suggest whatever is right for your particular portfolio.

+ **Your financial advisor should be experienced**. In general, the more years of experience your advisor has, the better. Although you may be more comfortable initially working with someone your own age (especially if you're very young), or you may want to give a new advisor who's just starting out a chance, that's not really the best criteria to use. Instead, you want someone who has at least five years of experience.

+ **Your financial advisor should personally handle your portfolio**. The flip side of the experience issue is that as some advisors become more successful and take on more clients, they hire support staff to help them with their workloads. That assistance is fine, provided it's administrative work, such as answering phones, taking messages, researching, handling correspondence, and filing, and not the actual work of choosing and monitoring your investments. Obviously, you want the person or team you hire and trust to be doing the work he or she promised to do for you. That said, it's still important to develop a good relationship with every-one who works alongside your advisor.

✦ **Your financial advisor should be someone you trust**. This may seem obvious, but in the aftermath of scandals involving scoundrels like Bernie Madoff, it's worth stating. It's your hard-earned money that's at stake, which means it's also your future and peace of mind at stake. It's a good idea to ask a friend, your lawyer, your accountant, or one of your other professional advisors for a recommendation. Get several rec-ommendations from different people. Ask your friends what they like and don't like about their own financial advisors.

What to Ask Potential Financial Advisors

Ask potential advisors how much time they spend on monitoring investments and talking to clients they already have. You might also ask them how much time they devote to finding new clients, since marketing the business is something that every indepen-dent businessperson obviously needs to do. But you want to make sure their work finding new clients doesn't detract from their ac-tually doing the work for existing clients.

As a general rule of thumb, your financial advisor should spend at least eight to ten hours a day directly serving the needs of existing clients. You're probably thinking, "Wow, that's a lot of time! How could anyone possibly have any time or energy left over for anything else?" That's exactly the point though. For advi-sors to be knowledgeable about what's happening in the markets and the economy in general, they need to spend most of the day researching and monitoring the markets and communicating with clients about what's best for their individual portfolios. Note: many advisors use email as their primary means of communica-tion, which is fine. It's not necessary to talk to your advisor, as long as you're receiving the information you need.

> **Quick and Dirty Tip**
>
> Don't simply choose the financial advisor who's the least expensive, because like many other things in life, you may get what you pay for.

As mentioned earlier, it's a good idea to get recommendations for financial advisors. Before hiring one, you should interview the advisors who've been recommended. If an advisor has written anything—articles, books, or even newsletters—take a look at them to get a feel for his or her level of experience and knowledge. Written materials offer a form of evidence for what an advisor has advised in the past. If one of the advisors has documented proof that he or she recommended investing in something that later paid off, for example, that's helpful to know. Finally, trust your gut. If you're not comfortable talking to an advisor, that's not a good sign—no matter how great that advisor's track record might be.

Good Luck!

We've covered a lot in this book. We started with the investing basics, talked about how to understand what's going on in the economy and with the markets, and explained how you can apply different types of analysis to potential investments to identify and select the smartest ones. If you do decide to work with a financial advisor, you'll be a knowledgeable client. You'll be better able to understand the advice your advisor gives you, to ask informed questions, and to truly work together to become a winning investor. Good luck!

P.S. If you need me, you can find me at www.winninginvestor.quickanddirtytips.com, where my weekly podcasts and corresponding web articles answer common investing questions. I'll look forward to hearing from you!

Glossary:
Quick and Dirty Definitions
of Key Concepts

asset: Any item of value owned by a business. A company lists its assets on a balance sheet, and the total assets are eventually reduced by the company's total liabilities.

balance sheet: A snapshot of a company's financial picture at a specific point in time. Sometimes called the *statement of financial position*, the balance sheet shows the company's assets (on the left side of the statement), and its liabilities, or debt (on the right side). The company's assets are listed from top to bottom in the sequence of most liquid to least liquid—that is, the assets that can be converted to cash fastest are listed first, and the assets that are more difficult to convert to cash follow. Similarly, the company's liabilities are listed from top to bottom in the sequence in which they need to be paid off, beginning with those due first.

bar chart: A type of stock chart in which each day is represented by a vertical line, or bar. The top of the bar represents a particular stock's high value that day, and the bottom represents the low value. Small horizontal lines on the left and/or right of the bar reflect the opening and closing prices of that stock.

bear market: Market condition in which investment prices decline over a prolonged period of time. Bear markets are usually associated with recession.

bond: One of the four main investing vehicles, which is basically an IOU. There are many different types of bonds. When you buy a bond, you're lending your money to a company or government, which promises to pay back the loan at some date in the future, together with the interest on that loan. You make money by earning the interest. A bond matures, or comes due, a certain amount of time after it's issued, depending on the time period set by the issuing company. Usually, the longer the term, or time period, the more interest you'll earn.

bond rating: A measurement of a bond's relative safety for investing and its potential to default.

bull market: Market condition in which investment prices are consistently rising in value. Consumer confidence is generally high during bull markets, which are usually indicative of an economic boom or period of economic recovery following a recession.

"buy and hold" investing strategy: Long-term investing strategy in which an investor purchases a stock and holds it over a long period of time, regardless of market fluctuations. Also known as the "Sleeping Beauty" portfolio.

candle stick charts: Type of stock chart similar to a bar chart in structure except that each day's trading for a particular stock looks like a candle with a wick coming out of each end.

capacity utilization percentage: An industrial production report which estimates how much of the nation's capital stock is being used to produce goods.

capital gains: The increase in the value of a stock or investment that sold in a given year over the cost basis.

cash flow statement: A report that all public companies (companies that sell stock to the public) must issue to their shareholders quarterly. The statement shows how much cash is flowing in and out of a company, and thus reveals the company's short-term viability and its ability to pay its bills.

Certified Financial Planner (CFP®): A financial advisor who has been certified by the International Board of Standards and Practices for Certified Financial Planners.

coincident indicator: An economic indicator that moves in conjunction with the economy and shows what's happening in the present economy.

commodities: Basic goods you can invest in, such as corn and energy, that are uniform among producers.

congestion: A price pattern in which no discernible trend emerges for a particular stock or market.

consumer confidence: A measurement of how consumers feel about the current, or future, state of the economy. Consumer confidence is usually a strong indicator of the economy's strength as a whole.

consumer price index (CPI): A government report measuring price changes for a fixed basket of consumer goods and services. The CPI report is used to track inflation trends.

contraction phase: The phase in an economic cycle where economic activity begins to slow down. Severe contraction phases may lead to a recession.

corporate bonds: A type of bond issued by a corporation that's usually riskier than government or municipal bonds. The quality of a corporate bond is directly tied to the financial strength of the company issuing it.

correction: A market condition in which the prevailing trend reverses; most often used to refer to a downtrend.

currency risk: The risk on foreign investments caused by fluctuating worldwide currency-exchange rates. If you own an investment in another country, when you sell that investment and convert your profits back to your local currency (for example, euros to U.S. dollars), there may be a loss or gain (in addition to whatever you lost or gained on the investment itself), depending on the currency exchange rate at the time you sell and convert.

diversification: A way to manage risk by spreading it out among multiple investments in your portfolio. It can mean holding different kinds of stocks instead of just one or investing in bonds or mutual funds in addition to stocks. The theory behind diversification is that it will help protect you if one type of investment loses money, because you'll have other types of investments that are hopefully making money, thus balancing out the loss.

dividends: Payments given to the shareholders of a company, usually on a quarterly basis, as a way for corporations to "share" their profits and provide an incentive to remain invested.

dollar cost averaging: An investing strategy in which you invest the same amount of money on a regular basis no matter what the market or investment is doing.

Dow Jones Industrial Average (DJIA): Made up of thirty stocks, the Dow is one of the most widely followed stock indexes in the world. It is named after Charles Dow, who was a cofounder of Dow Jones & Company, a publishing and financial information firm started in 1882. Though the word *Industrial* is in its name, today the DIJA includes companies from many sectors of the economy: financial services such as American Express, restaurants such as McDonald's, technology such as Microsoft, pharmaceuticals like Pfizer, and retail like Walmart.

downtrend: A condition in which the market experiences a series of lower price lows and lower price highs.

earnings per share (EPS): A ratio used to evaluate how much profit a stock has earned. This ratio is probably the most widely used by stock analysts (and any investor doing fundamental analysis of a stock) because it looks at profit per share, instead of overall profit. However, this ratio is more useful when you compare the current figure to one from a previous time period (either the last quarter of the year or even a year before). When you compare EPS figures over time, you can determine the rate of growth of a company's earnings.

economic cycle: The long-term pattern of an economy. The cycle has four stages: the growth stage, the peak stage, the contraction stage, and the trough stage.

efficient market theory: The extent to which securities prices reflect what is known and promptly adjust to what becomes known. Even with the advent of technology, an active press, and easily accessible online trading, there is still an ongoing debate about market efficiency.

exchange-traded fund (ETF): An investing vehicle. It is similar to a mutual fund in that it's made up of different securities, but it is also different because it trades like a stock on an exchange. ETFs are more flexible than mutual funds because you can buy and sell shares of ETFs throughout the day, taking advantage of inter-day changes in the market. ETF fees are often lower than mutual fund fees because ETFs don't need to be actively managed.

expansion: A period of economic growth.

flat market: A market condition in which there is neither an upward nor downward trend.

Forex market: a foreign exchange market used to facilitate trade between countries; primarily used for currency exchanges.

fundamental analysis: One of the three main types of analysis, it focuses on the value of the investment, not the price. Investors determine the value by researching and evaluating a company's earnings history, balance sheet, management, product line, and other factors that will affect its overall profitability and growth.

global fund: An international mutual fund that invests primarily in foreign companies, but may also invest in companies based in the U.S.

gross domestic product (GDP): A measurement of the value of economic activity of a country. The GDP of the United States is the monetary value of all the goods and services the country produces during a specific period of time.

growth stocks: Stocks that are typically more earnings-based—when investors look at growth stocks, they generally look to the ongoing growth of earnings, rather than the overall stability of the company.

hedging: A financial strategy used to minimize risk. Options or an inverse ETF is often used.

income statement: A statement that shows a company's financial performance during a specific time frame. The typical accounting period is every three months (aka, a quarter, because it's a quarter of a year). The income statement, or report, shows the company's net profit or loss during this period, among other details.

indicators: Certain pieces of information, like consumer confidence, that act as clues into the state of the economy.

inflation risk: The risk of the purchasing power of the dollar diminishing over time. In general, the cost of everything we buy tends to increase: for example, in the early 1900s a loaf of bread cost only 5¢, whereas today it can cost $2 to $3.

international fund: An international mutual fund that invests exclusively in foreign companies.

international index fund: An international mutual fund that tries to track results of a particular foreign market equity index.

inverse ETF: An exchange-traded fund that gains value as the market goes down because it is structured to make money when stocks decline.

IPO (initial public offering): The first stock sold by a private company that is going public—that is, the company will now trade stock on a public exchange. IPOs are risky investments because the companies are usually newer and lack proven track records.

junk bond: A term for a low-quality (below investment grade) corporate bond. Junk bonds may return a high interest rate but carry a higher risk of default.

lagging indicator: An economic indicator that changes after the economy has already begun to follow a particular trend in a cycle.

large-cap companies: Companies that are usually valued at over $5 billion in terms of market capitalization.

leading indicator: An economic indicator that precedes an economic trend.

liabilities: Any obligations a company has to pay, including bills and debts, as well as the interest and principal payments on bonds. A company's liabilities are listed on its balance sheet.

line chart: A type of stock chart comprised of dots that have been connected by a line, representing a stock's closing price over a period of time.

liquidity risk: How easily you can buy and sell an investment. A stock that is difficult to sell isn't liquid.

market capitalization: The value of the outstanding shares of a company's stock—that is, the number of shares issued and owned by the public multiplied by the company's current stock price.

market efficiency: The theory that everything an investor needs to know about a prospective investment is already factored into the price of that company's stock.

market timing: An attempt to buy or sell investments and/or enter and exit the market at the right time by anticipating when prices are going to rise or fall.

micro-cap companies: Companies that are generally under $250 million in terms of market capitalization.

mid-cap companies: Companies valued from around $1 billion to $5 billion in terms of market capitalization.

moving averages: The average price of a stock over a given period of time.

municipal bond: Bond that was issued by a state, city, or local government.

mutual fund: An investment vehicle where many shareholders pool their money in order to invest in a diversified portfolio of securities (stocks, bonds, or anything that represents financial value). Instead of having to research and choose specific stocks, bonds, or other investment vehicle, investors pool their money along with others into a conglomeration of investments that are chosen and managed by a professional mutual-fund manager.

NASDAQ (National Association of Securities Dealers Automated Quotations): One of the biggest markets in the United States where stocks are bought and sold. NASDAQ is an electronically traded market and not a physical location.

New York Stock Exchange (NYSE): One of the biggest markets in the United States. It's an auction-based exchange, where specialists in specific stocks take orders for buying and selling shares. The NYSE is an actual place, located in Lower Manhattan.

P/E ratio: A calculation of a company's stock price (P) divided by that company's earnings per share (E). P/E ratio indicates how much investors are willing to pay for the stock, as compared to that company's earnings.

PEG ratio: A calculation of a company's P/E ratio divided by the company's expected per-share earnings growth over the next few years.

price-to-book ratio: A calculation that compares a stock's current market price to its book value, which is simply the company's assets minus its liabilities.

producer price index (PPI): A government report used to evaluate wholesale price levels in the economy.

quantitative analysis: An approach to assessing investments that uses filters and screens to easily narrow down a huge list of available investments to those you may want to research further.

rally market: A condition in which the market is in an upward trend.

REIT (real estate investment trusts): Pronounced "reets." REITs are pooled investments in apartments or in commercial buildings, including office buildings, nursing homes, hospitals, shopping malls, or other diversified property. REITs are actively traded on a stock exchange like the NYSE, and they provide the potential for above average income through a dividend.

resistance level: The price at which a stock has a limited ability to go higher.

revenue bond: A form of municipal bond that repays bond holders with income from public works projects or tolls.

risk tolerance: The amount of psychological pain you can deal with when investing.

S&P 500: A closely watched stock index made up of stocks from 500 companies. The S&P 500 index traditionally consists of bigger companies, and it includes many of the popular and well-known stocks that are generally traded, such as Aetna insurance (AET), DuPont Chemicals (DD), Hasbro Toys (HAS), IBM (IBM), Macy's (M), PepsiCo (PEP), Sherwin-Williams (SHW), and Yahoo! (YHOO). Many portfolio managers, investment advisors, and mutual fund managers use the S&P 500 index as a benchmark to track their performance—to compare how their specific investments are doing versus the S&P 500. Because the S&P 500 index consists of 500 companies' stocks, it's much more representative of the stock market as a whole than the Dow.

screen: A set of criteria used by investors to narrow down the list of investments they would like to examine further. Also called a filter.

sell stop: Automatic order to sell a stock once the price reaches a specified number.

sideways market: A condition in which a market exhibits no discernible trend (also called a rangebound market).

small-cap companies: Companies that are usually valued between $500,000 and $1 billion in terms of market capitalization.

stock: An investing vehicles. When you purchase stocks, you buy shares in a company, thereby giving you an ownership interest in the company.

stock index: A grouping of stocks that have certain similar characteristics and can be tracked as one unit. An index can be made up of companies from a specific sector (health care, real estate, and so on), a specific market size, a certain geographic area, or type of investment. Two of the main U.S. stock indexes are the Dow Jones Industrial Average and the S&P 500. Though you can't purchase shares of an index, you can invest in funds, such as ETFs, that mirror the performance of certain indexes.

support level: The price at which a stock price has limited ability to go any lower.

technical analysis: A type of analysis that tracks historical prices of an investment, so investors can discover and exploit price trends. Technical analysis is used primarily with stocks, but it can also be used to forecast market indexes such as the S&P 500, industries, sectors, bonds, currencies, commodities, and so forth. To technical analysts, price is the only thing that matters.

Treasury Inflation Protected Securities (TIPS): Bonds issued by the U.S. government which pay interest every six months and pay the bond's principal when it matures, plus an additional amount depending on the rate of inflation.

uptrend: A condition in which the market experiences a series of higher price highs and higher price lows

U.S. Treasury bonds: Bonds that are sold and backed by the federal government.

value stocks: An example may be stocks from companies with a higher book value—that is, the company's assets minus its liabilities. The company's earnings might not be steadily growing, but they still may be quite profitable. Value stocks tend to pay dividends, payments generally given quarterly to shareholders as a way for companies to "share" their profits.

volatile market: A market defined by large, unpredictable price movements.

Acknowledgments

Writing a book is not easy. It takes patience, hard work, and a great deal of support from others. Whether it is a new idea or a take on an old one, the metamorphosis from initial to final stage takes more than one attempt. From writes and rewrites to proofs to edits (and back again) there are many people whom I would like to personally thank for helping me through all stages.

My original contact with the Quick and Dirty Tips was Mignon—Grammar Girl. We developed a great friendship when I took over as Money Girl during a period in between hosts. Mignon was the original force behind *The Winning Investor*—THANKS!

The editorial team that assisted in all aspects of the writing: Ruth, Corey, and Emily—you are a great team. Then there was Richard, who kept me going with constant encouragement and a well needed push, more often than I like to admit. Kevin, my right and left hand is hard to thank, as no amount of thanks will ever be enough for all of the hard work, loyalty, and friendship he has provided as this book was written. Even so, Thanks!

Of course, my family has been terrific. Lauren, Erica, and Brett, my children, have been a great source of encouragement and incentive. My hope is that they will be able to invest wisely over their lives and use the lessons inside of this book to become winning investors on their own.

Finally, my wife, Jill, is a constant source of ideas and inspiration. Thank you for being my better half and always reminding me about the importance of family and friends.

To the readers and listeners of *The Disciplined Investor* and *Winning Investor*—you are the heart and soul of this entire effort. Thank you. You are all winners in my book!

About the Author

ANDREW HOROWITZ is the host of *The Winning Investor* podcast, author of *The Disciplined Investor: Essential Strategies for Success,* and a Certified Financial Planner® who has been managing money for individual and corporate clients since the late 1980s. He is president of the investment advisory firm Horowitz & Company and has written frequently for the MSN Money Blog and for AOL Finance. He is also the former host of *The Money Doctor,* a radio call-in show.

Various local and national media often seek out Andrew as an authority on diverse investment management issues. He has been featured in such newspapers as *The Wall Street Journal, USA Today, Barron's,* the *Financial Times,* the *Miami Herald, The New York Times,* and the *Sun Sentinel* to name a few. Andrew has also appeared on CNBC, Fox News, and *The Jon Stewart Show.* He lives in South Florida.

Index

Quick and Dirty Tips™
Helping you do things better.

"The sixth-grade teacher you wish you had."—*USA TODAY*

"Adams's peppy tone and highly organized, sensible advice deliver a clear-cut plan for financial literacy."
—*PUBLISHERS WEEKLY*

"Robbins' advice is sensible and practical."—*MIAMI HERALD*

AVAILABLE MARCH:
Nutrition Diva's Secrets for a Healthy Diet: What to Eat, What to Avoid, and What to Stop Worrying About

AVAILABLE AUGUST:
Math Dude's Quick and Dirty Guide to Algebra

St. Martin's Griffin